Second Language Practice

Multilingual Matters

Please contact us for the latest book information:
Multilingual Matters Ltd, Frankfurt Lodge, Clevedon Hall,
Victoria Road, Clevedon, Avon, England, BS21 7SJ.

Second Language Practice

Classroom Strategies for Developing Communicative Competence

Edited by
Georges Duquette

MULTILINGUAL MATTERS LTD
Clevedon • Philadelphia • Adelaide

95-139981

Library of Congress Cataloging in Publication Data

Second Language Practice: Classroom Strategies for Developing Communicative Competence/Edited by Georges Duquette.
Includes bibliographical references and index.
1. Language and languages–Study and teaching. 2. Communicative competence.
I. Duquette, Georges.
P53.S3918   1995
418'.007–dc20   95-30458

British Library Cataloguing in Publication Data

A CIP catalogue record for this book is available from the British Library.

ISBN 1-85359-306-0 (hbk)
ISBN 1-85359-305-2 (pbk)

Multilingual Matters Ltd

UK: Frankfurt Lodge, Clevedon Hall, Victoria Road, Clevedon, Avon BS21 7SJ.
USA: 1900 Frost Road, Suite 101, Bristol, PA 19007, USA.
Australia: P.O. Box 6025, 83 Gilles Street, Adelaide, SA 5000, Australia.

Typeset by Archetype, Stow-on-the-Wold.
Printed and bound in Great Britain by the Cromwell Press.

Contents

Introduction

Over the past 25 years, many theorists specialising in second language acquisition have promoted the communicative approach. Their arguments have been very convincing, but many school boards and teachers remain unsure as to how to implement this approach in the classroom; they do not know which specific skills should be developed, at which levels, or what strategies should be used. They need to see more continuity in their programmes, to relate strategies to outcome expectations, to observe and verify from time to time an increase in competence in their students, to understand how one element of a programme relates to another.

Because teachers are practical people, they need a publication which offers them ideas on how to develop second language skills in their students at various levels of competence development. Second and foreign language programmes at the university level designed to develop target language skills are generally distributed along a five level span, from the L2 learner who has no or few skills (level 1) to the learner who has sufficiently mastered the target language to successfully follow university courses in that language (level 5). For this reason, the chapters in this book are targeted to those levels. Any adjustment can then be made by school boards or universities to meet the needs of other students, keeping in mind their age, background and social status, L1 and L2 comprehension, and proficiency skills. Here's how the levels break down.

Basic (levels 1 and 2)
Intermediate (levels 3 and 4)
Advanced (level 5)

As pointed out by Baker (1993), there is more than one way to get students to develop communicative competence. There is no single or simple recipe or programme which will do the job entirely, but we do need to get started. We now know enough about the acquisition process that we can provide clear theoretical directions and practical examples of strategies consistent with second and foreign language theory for classroom implementation. Innovative teachers and administrators can then continue the process, add or substract to the repertoire of strategies, in accordance with their student needs.

For clarification purposes, communicative competence in this book means having the necessary 'know how' to understand and respond to different situations which arise.

This definition is based in large part on Krashen and Terrell's natural hypothesis theory (1983), the emphasis being on acquisition rather than learning, as well as Krashen's updated comprehensible input theory (1994). This is indeed an important notion. After all, how can there by student output if comprehensible input is kept to a minimum? How can there be real world knowledge and pragmatic competence if school knowledge and academic performance are emphasised? As a result, these publications have provided the guiding principles for this volume.

The book is also inspired by Seliger's notion of strategy as 'superordinate, abstract, constant and long-term processes' (1991:37). It attempts to offer teachers and students a number of strategies which are transferable from one situation to another and may prove helpful in the real world.

Finally, it is recognised that after the input, there are real context and culture-based expectations with regard to the output as suggested by Majhanovich in her chapter (in this book). These expectations are real and students will encounter them naturally. Correcting errors is not an easy task and it requires some teach preparation. Over-correction slows down and can even stifle communication altogether; no correction at all may lead to some fossilisation of errors. Calvé (1992) addresses this problem and provides strategies to deal with it, as pointed out by Demers and Bérubé in their chapter (also in this book).

This publication should interest elementary and secondary level classroom teachers and administrators, professors of modern languages and second language educators, professors and students in faculties of education, specialists in English as a second language, French as a second language, modern languages, heritage and multicultural education, etc.

A second language class should be both fun and worthwhile, leading to communication experiences both in and outside of class which are personally rewarding for students.

References

Baker, C. (1993) *Foundations of Bilingual Education and Bilingualism*. Clevedon, England: Multilingual Matters.

Calvé, P. (1992) Corriger ou ne pas corriger, là n'est pas la question. *The Canadian Modern Language Review/La Revue canadienne des langues vivantes* 48, (3), 458–71.

Krashen, S.D. (1994) The case for free voluntary reading. *The Canadian Modern Language Review*, 50 (1), 72–82.

Krashen, S.D. and Terrell, T. (1983) *The Natural Approach: Language Acquisition in the Classroom*. Oxford: Pergamon.

Seliger, H. (1991) Strategy and tactics in second language acquisition. In L. Malavé and G. Duquette (eds) *Language, Culture, and Cognition: A Collection of Studies in First and Second Language Acquisition*. Clevedon, England: Multilingual Matters.

Performance Goals

To increase communicative competence in students, this book has set a number of goals. Classroom students should be able to use:

(1) Comprehension skills through listening and viewing.
(2) Oral communication skills in context for problem-solving purposes.
(3) Reading comprehension skills for both necessity and pleasure.
(4) Skills in determining level, variety, appropriateness, and register of language according to group norms and social expectations.
(5) Skills in communicating thoughts and feelings in writing.
(6) Skills in improving the structure of the written form.

Acknowledgements

I would like to acknowledge the help, support and cooperation I have received from the team at Multilingual Matters. I have always appreciated their competence, high level of professionalism, as well as their personal openness and understanding. Please do continue the good work.

I also wish to thank Diana Luerle-Collili and Léanne Génier for their assistance in reviewing and commenting upon the articles received for publication.

Finally, my sincere thanks to all the authors who have submitted articles for this book. Their contribution has been appreciated.

G.D.

Biographical Notes on the Contributing Authors

GUYLAINE BÉRUBÉ is currently teaching at Peace Arch Elementary School (Surrey District School Board) in White Rock, British Columbia, Canada. She has taught language skills to students of various levels (elementary to university).

ANNE BOURQUE taught FSL and French immersion with the Haldimand and Halton Boards of Education and spent five years teaching in Baden-Sollingen, Germany, for the Canadian Department of National Defense before moving to British Columbia in 1989. She is currently on secondment to Simon Fraser University from the Langley School District with the Department of Education and Undergraduate Programs where she is teaching a methodology course in Social studies for Immersion teachers.

GAIL C. BRITANIK teaches English to Speakers of Other Languages at the Highbridge Community Life Center in Bronx, NY. She has a Master's degree and TESOL certification from the University of Pittsburg where she taught courses in the English Language Institute. Ms Britanik has also taught survival and workplace ESL courses for refugees. Her major interest is applying the thought of Paulo Freire and Myles Horton to ESL teaching and learning.

MARY CALDER teaches in the English Language Programme at the University of Alberta in Edmonton. She has taught ESL for the North York Board of Education and the University of Regina. While teaching classes in all areas of ESL, she developed a particular interest in writing. Recently she became involved as a teacher-researcher looking into the writing development of ESL students in her own classes. She is a facilitator with the South Saskatchewan Writing Project.

MICHELLE CLÉMENT is a teacher of French as a first language to intermediate and senior high school students. She holds BA and BEd Degrees, an Ontario Teacher's Certificate, as well as an additional qualification to teach French as a first language to senior-level students.

After modifying the teaching unit on the short story for her classroom needs, she adapted it to share it further with second language teachers.

PIERRE DEMERS has been involved in L2 teaching for over 20 years, as a teacher, a consultant, a researcher and an administrator. He is now Assistant Professor in the Department of French of the University of New Brunswick, Fredericton, New Brunswick, Canada.

JOSEPH E. DICKS is Assistant Professor at Université Sainte-Anne, Novia Scotia. He was previously Project Officer at the French Second Language Teacher Education Centre of the University of New Brunswick where he worked on the development of the Maritime Oral Communication Assessment Portfolio. Professor Dicks has conducted research in the area of experiential and analytical features of second lanaguage classrooms. He has extensive teaching experience in French as a second language.

GEORGES DUQUETTE (PhD, State University of New York at Buffalo) was born in Canada and received his early education in Northern Ontario. He taught English and French both as a first and second language at the elementary and secondary (11 years) school levels. Later, he taught classroom methodology and second language university courses at the graduate and undergraduate levels (10 years). His publications on bilingual and minority language education have appeared in refereed and non-refereed journals in Canada, the US and Europe. He is, with Lilliam Malavé, co-editor of (1991) *Language, Culture and Cognition* (Multilingual Matters) and author of (1992) *Stratégies et méthodes pour l'enseignement au secondaire* (Les éditions Soleil Publications). He is currently Associate Professor at the School of Education, Laurentian University.

WILLIAM T. FAGAN, Professor at the University of Alberta, Edmonton, Alberta, has a PhD from the University of Alberta and also studied at the University of Toronto and the University of Michigan. He has been a teacher of all grade levels, and the recipient of the International Reading Association Outstanding Dissertation of the year, the National Council of Teachers of English Promising Research Award, and the Alberta McCalla Research Professorship. His present research interests include literacy development, adult literacy, and second language learning.

GLENWOOD IRONS is the Associate Professor in the Department of Applied Language Studies and Program in Communication Studies at Brock University. He is also founder and past director of the Department. His publications include *Second Language Acquisition: Selected Readings in Theory and Practice; Make Changes Make a Difference* (with Sima Paribakht); *Gender, Language, and Myth: Essays on Popular Narrative, Feminism in*

Women's Detective Fiction; and *La phonétique comparée du français et de l'anglais nord américains: tome 1; Les sons* (with luc Ostiguy and Robert Sarrasin).

SYLVAIN JACQUES arrived in British Columbia in 1985 and has taught for the Surrey School District since then. He also worked as a Language Consultant for the district from 1990 to 1992. From 1992 to 1994 he was on secondment to Simon Fraser University as a Faculty Associate with the Professional Development Program in the Faculty of Education. For the past eight summers, he has been working with the University of British Columbia's bursary program in Québec City. He continues to facilitate workshops in second language acquisition all over British Columbia and in other parts of Canada and continues to teach methodology courses in second language instruction in Simon Fraser University. Currently he is teaching a grade 4/5 Immersion class in Surrey BC.

JUMIN HU holds an MEd Degree from the University of Western Ontario. Born in China, he received his BEd Degree in English language and literature from Anhui University and an MA Degree in English linguistics from Xiamen University. Before coming to Canada, he taught English as a foreign language at Hefei University of technology for a total of five years. He has contributed a number of articles to journals and conferences, including the *Western Journal of Graduate Reseach* and the *Comparative and International Education Society Newsletter.* Hu is now a PhD candidate in Teaching English as a Second Language at the University of British Columbia.

DIANE LATAILLE-DÉMORÉ is a professor at the School of Education, Laurentian University, in Sudbury, Ontario. Diane has taught Second Language classes at all levels and Second Language pedagogy at the pre-service level. She is presently teaching general methodology, again at the pre-service level.

RAYMOND LEBLANC holds a Doctorat de 3e cycle (Linguistique) from the Université d'Aix-Marseille. He is currently employed by the University of Ottawa where he is a Professor at the Second Language Institute of that university. He is also currently Director of the SLI. A teacher of both French and English as second languages during his career, he is involved in the MEd and the BA programmes in Second Language Teaching at the University of Ottawa. Author of a number of titles in language teaching materials, he has also published and edited a number of articles and books on various aspects of language teaching and testing. He was the Director of the National Core French Study.

SUZANNE MAJHANOVICH (PhD, University of Colorado) is an associate professor and Chair of the Curriculum Division at the Faculty of Education, the University of Western Ontario. She has taught second language methodology in both the pre-service and graduate programmes and is the author of a series of intermediate and senior level French as a second language texts, as well as a number of articles on second language acquisition, language policy, and teacher education for second language teachers. She is also active in the Comparative and International Education Society of Canada.

TED MILTENBERGER is a professor of theatre arts at the American University of Paris and an active member of the International Theatre Schools' Association.

JOAN NETTEN is a Professor in the Faculty of Education at Memorial University of Newfoundland where she has been responsible for the development and coordination of the French second language teacher education programme at both the undergraduate and graduate levels. She has also been responsible for the evaluation of the French immersion programmes in the province from their inception until recently. She served as Consultant, French Programmes, Evaluation and Research, and as Assistant Director, Language Programmes, in the Newfoundland Department of Education, has been a member of several ministerial committees established to study French first and second language education in the province, and represented the government in negotiations for French first language schooling in St John's. Currently, she teaches courses, both graduate and undergraduate, related to second language acquisition and the curriculum and methodology of French second language programmes. Her research interests include French immersion pedagody and classroom processes and their relationship to second language development, in which areas she has published a number of articles.

GISÈLE PAINCHAUD holds a PhD (Adult Education) from the Université de Montréal. She is a Professor in the Department of Learning and Instruction and is currently Dean of the Faculty of Education of the Université de Montréal. She has taught French as a second language to adults and has been involved with the training of language teachers for a number of years. She has published extensively on language teaching, language testing and literacy in Canada and abroad and she was responsible for the Language Syllabus in the National Core French Study.

CHRISTINA BRATT PAULSTON is Professor in the Department of Linguistics at the University of Pittsburgh and also Director of the English

Language Institute at the University. She received a doctorate from Columbia University in 1966. Prior to working at the University of Pittsburgh, Professor Paulston has taught English as a second language in Morocco, Sweden, India and Peru, from seventh grade to University level as well as in high school English and French in Minnesota. She has published in the fields of language teaching, teacher training, language planning, bilingual education, and socio-linguistics. She was president of TESOL in 1976 and trustee of the Center for Applied Linguistics from 1976–81. In 1980 she received the Research Review Award from the American Educational Research Association.

Some major publications include (1994) *Linguistic Minorities in Multilingual Settings: Implications for Language Policy* (Benjamins); (1992) *Linguistic and Communicative Competence: Topics in ESL* (Multilingual Matters); (1992) *Sociolinguistic Perspectives on Bilingual Education* (Multilingual Matters); (1988) *International Handbook on Bilingualism and Bilingual Education* (Greenwood Press); (1983) *Swedish Research and Debate about Bilingualism* (National Swedish Board of Education); (1980) *Trends in Language Teaching and Bilingual Education* (SEAMEO Regional Language Centre); (1980) *English as a Second Language* (US National Education Association); (1980) *Bilingual Education: Issues and Theories* (Newbury House); (1980) *Teaching English to Speakers of Other Languages in the US, 1976: A Dipstick Paper* (Center for Applied Linguistics); with Bruder, M.N. (1976) *Procedures and Techniques in Teaching English as a Second Language* (Winthrop).

JANETTE PLANCHAT-FERGUSON has taught French as a second language in both core French and early immersion programmes for a number of years. She has also taught French as a second language to adult learners with the Division of Continuing Studies at Memorial University. She has been a member of several curriculum working groups developing teaching guides for the FSL programmes in the Province of Newfoundland, and has served as an Educational Consultant for the early French immersion programmes with the Newfoundland Department of Education. She has presented workshops on the use of improvisational drama in enhancing second language production at conferences of both the Canadian Association of Second Language Teachers and l'Association canadienne des professeurs d'immersion.

SALLY REHORICK is Senior Research Associate in the French Second Language Teacher Education Centre at the University of New Brunswick. She was Project Director for the development of the Maritime Oral Communication Assessment Portfolio. Professor Rehorick conducts research in second language assessment and teacher effectiveness and is Co-editor of the *Canadian Modern Language Review*.

HANA SVAB is a graduate of the Faculty of Education of Laurentian University and The School of Translators and Interpreters of the University of Ottawa. She speaks and writes half a dozen languages and has taught English and French as foreign languages in Italy, Switzerland, the Czech Republic and Ethiopia. She is completing a Master's Degree in Curriculum and Teaching in Europe with Michigan State University and has recently accepted an ESL coordinator's position for Hong Kong.

1 Strategies for Beginning Listening Comprehension

GLENWOOD IRONS

This chapter outlines the importance of listening comprehension over the other skills, particularly at the early levels of second language learning. Using, among others, Asher's early 1970's project which resulted in the well-known Learning Another Language Through Actions, *Pierre Capretz's* French in Action *series, and Anderson and Lynch's* Listening, *this author examines the essential features used in a 'listening approach' to teaching a second language. Winitz's early 1980's findings, published as the* Comprehension Approach to Foreign Language Teaching, *and University of Ottawa's 'subject matter language teaching' project, with Stephen Krashen, are also briefly assessed. Finally, using language courses at the author's university, some classroom strategies for incorporating a listening-based syllabus are proposed.*

Introduction

Listening comprehension has finally come into its own as a recognised and separate skill to be taught as such in the language teaching environment. No longer is listening comprehension relegated to the drudgery of cassette tapes in the language lab, or *dictées* in the classroom: it is now clearly recognised as a skill which should be accomplished along with speaking, writing and reading. There is little doubt that this has been brought about by psycholinguists, applied linguists and language teachers alike. But the main thrust in this direction has been provided by early researchers and teachers of the comprehension approach to second language learning.

Pioneers of comprehension-based instruction like James Asher (1977), Harris Winitz (1981), Tracy Terrell (1983), and Anderson and Lynch (1988) have altered forever the have-not status of listening comprehension. Asher, Terrell, Winitz and others have even argued for the *priority* of listening comprehension over all other language skills. Listening, they say, is the key to progress and success in speaking, reading and writing. And while most of the work done by Asher, Winitz and Terrell focuses on improvements in comprehension-based language teaching at the primary and secondary levels, Courchene *et al.*, (1992), as well as Irons and Paribakht (1992), for example, examine recent strategies for teaching comprehension to university students.

As it turns out, one of the strongest arguments in favour of teaching language skills through listening comprehension is the famous Canadian experiment known as French Immersion. Supported by researchers, students, teachers, parents and even administrators, French Immersion in its essence teaches the language via comprehension of subject matter. And while there is a growing body of criticism against immersion as a method (see for example Hammerly, 1989), it continues to entice more parents and students than there are places available. In fact, its success at bilingual institutions like Canada's University of Ottawa has recently been recorded for posterity in Courchene *et al.'s Comprehension Based Second Language Teaching*.

Nevertheless, the apparent 'coming of age' which the teaching of listening comprehension as a skill has enjoyed has not made the techniques as readily available as one might assume. In the first place, immersion methods are not available to all language learners, nor are they necessarily desirable, not least because of the expense, but also because of the age at which students normally begin, and because of the time required to progress through immersion. The same problem obtains for the Content-based and Sheltered language programmes at the University of Ottawa, the only institution in Canada where comprehension-based techniques are employed on a regular basis. In the second place, it is not always easy to commute the requirements of a listening comprehension text into classroom practice in a specific circumstance. Teachers may not be sold on the ideas presented in a given text on listening comprehension simply because they have not been schooled in the idea that listening is an identifiable language skill which can be taught as such. Finally, even when an educator is relatively interested in teaching comprehension as a skill, s/he often has difficulty convincing parents and students of its efficacy. As we all know, listening is not a skill whose mastery is easy to evaluate. Speaking, writing, and even reading are readily evaluated using the actual skill; a successful speaker speaks, writer writes, and reader reads in a relatively observable fashion. It is all too easy to take listening as a skill for granted *because* problematic and even successful listening is not all that easily observable.

These problems often limit the amount of time to which a language teacher is willing to commit to the teaching of comprehension. This was observed in the early 1970s by James Asher, a Professor of Psychology at San Jose State University, and the well-known 'originator' of the Total Physical Response (TPR) method for teaching languages (primarily at the secondary school level). Asher reasoned that only actual classroom success in language learning through comprehension-based techniques would enhance teacher interest. He set about devising a method which would employ listening comprehension skills at the same time that it would improve success rates among adolescent learners of the various languages available in the secondary school curriculum.

Documented in *Learning Another Language Through Actions*, a listening comprehension textbook published by Asher's own publishing house through eight printings and four editions, the TPR method requires that students begin their study of language through movement in response to commands given in the target language. In that way, obviously enough, the teacher is able to observe whether or not the students' comprehension is successful. This obviates the problem of evaluation through other language skills – for example, it avoids the usual requirement of having students respond in *writing* to oral language – and connects listening comprehension learning to movement, just as many other kinds of skill learning – swimming or bicycle riding, for example – are connected to 'doing'.

According to Asher, who supports his claims with an almost evangelical fervour, TPR increases the speed and accuracy with which students 'internalise' and ultimately *use* the language which they are learning. While academics are generally sceptical of Asher's claims, some high profile applied linguists, led by Stephen Krashen in the 1980s, have supported him. Although Krashen's own work has been subject to some rather severe critiques in the world of academic publishing (see for example Gregg, 1984), Asher's TPR seems to have fought the academic 'razor', rising time and again above the academic fray. For that reason, and simply because of the wide range of Asher's influence, *Learning Another Language Through Actions* is the first of three language programmes based on listening comprehension which we will briefly outline before suggesting an actual 14-week, one hour per day syllabus for teaching listening comprehension as part of a four-skill language programme.

Methods for Teaching Listening Comprehension

Learning Another Language Through Actions (James Asher)

One cannot help but be intrigued by this book and its author. Along with a 52-week (at approximately three hours per week) syllabus, we are given a lengthy discussion of Asher's personal reasons for writing the book, his perception of the problems faced in 'normal' language classes (which don't use his approach!), and a brief outline of his answers to questions most often posed by teachers who employ the text. Then comes the real cruncher: a plethora of neon-coloured flyers stuffed into the text and hawking the various products and books related to the Total Physical Response.

Even for those who are suspicious of the relatively non-acedemic, hard-sell approach taken by Asher's publishing house, Sky Oaks Productions, the text is considered by many to be a highly useful and effective preparation for focusing on listening comprehension as a method which eventually opens the student to success in all four language skills. Teachers are given a step-by-step introduction to TPR, then led quickly down the road to success in language teaching with specific classroom directions on a class-by-class basis, assuming that each class lasts for approximately three hours. Given a certain amount of ingenuity, most teachers will find enough material here to help them operate under the auspices of TPR for one full academic year in secondary school, or for an academic term in college/university. This kind of 'by the hand' approach should not be underestimated. It is successful *because* it gives us a great many ideas for day-to-day employment, something which most language texts only hint at.

The book is divided into four sections, the first of which gives some insight into the personality behind the creator. The second section includes useful theoretical background to the TPR method. This is particularly necessary for parents (and teachers!) who might be sceptical of basing a language programme on listening comprehension and delayed oral production. Of specific interest are the 10 or so pages which Asher devotes to describing 'why it works'. Part three predicts and then answers many of the questions which will be asked of instructors who opt for TPR. Beginning with questions which deal with summarising TPR, with the amount of research behind it, and with what work still needs to be done on the method, Asher answers a number of possible questions which have come out of the various uses to which his text has been put. The final and most important section of the book sets out 53 weeks of classroom lessons, beginning with 'how to orient and motivate the students', a highly relevant first lesson given the likelihood of resistance by both teachers and students in the early stages.

Along with the well-laid-out textbook for teachers, Asher's publishing house also produces a number of relevant games, student/teacher kits, slides and video pieces which may be used to accompany the text. This, in effect, sets out a complete teaching system which just about any language teacher can incorporate into or use as an entire syllabus. And it is worth repeating that the text and all the materials which Asher recommends for TPR are based on putting comprehension ahead of all other language skills in order to use that skill as an inroad to the others.

The main criticism that has been levelled at Asher (and followers such as Harris Winitz) is that TPR has rather limited application, specifically that it is only useful for short periods of time, and for relatively simple structures. It could be argued that certain complicated or abstract concepts – love and hate for example – cannot be learned by reacting to commands from an instructor. It might also be suggested that, while the method has undeniable uses in primary and secondary level language comprehension, it would face considerable resistance by adults, many of whom would find the requirements of movement on response to be childish. Further, it is well known that many students feel uncomfortable with delayed oral production since they see language production as an essential component of success.

Asher generally brushes such criticism aside. In fact, many of his followers (see, most recently, Glissan, 1993) make a strong case for using TPR at upper levels of language instruction, particularly to review grammatical functions and to strengthen certain facets of listening comprehension simply by increasing the semantic and grammatical complexity of the commands. Notwithstanding the controversy over TPR, it is generally admitted that a component of this method at the beginner level of language learning is certainly worth considering given the lack of success 'enjoyed' by most methods to date.

French in Action (Pierre Capretz)

While *French in Action* is, obviously enough, concerned with the teaching of only one language, the technique is of some interest to us here as it employs a comprehension centred approach. In fact, *French in Action* draws on what it calls a 'total immersion approach', and, as noted above, immersion as it was developed in Canada employs comprehension-based techniques on a large scale. Clearly, most language teachers would find such an idea intriguing since we are well aware that immersion usually implies an acquisition-like environment where motivation is very high because it is linked to some degree with survival in the target language classroom. It is also well known that the immersion teaching experience in Canadian primary and secondary schools employs a comprehension-based approach in the early stages wherein students are not required to produce the target language until they feel comfortable in doing so.

This 52-week programme for learning French is the highly successful version produced by Wellesley College, Harvard University and WGBH Boston, a subsidiary of American Public Television. The driving force behind the all-encompassing programme is Pierre Capretz, whose approach to language instruction is clearly comprehension based. Unlike the hard sell approach which Asher takes, Capretz uses a much more low-keyed come-on. Successful graduates of the series are interviewed and give their testaments on the first video-taped lesson. We hear how students have improved their French in ways only dreamed of in introductory language courses. Students claim to be able to carry on conversations beyond elementary naming of objects; they claim to be able to write letters to friends in French-speaking countries such as Switzerland; most importantly, they claim to be able to understand French as it is spoken by native speakers. But the most important feature of each testament is the enjoyment which students experienced, particularly compared to other programmes they have taken. Indeed, an eminent Harvard University anthropologist (of French culture) is interviewed, and claims that his own background was considerably less informed than that of students who follow the Capretz course. An added incentive for students (and teachers alike!) is the availability of the video sections of the course on public television in Australia, Canada, the UK and the United States.

The proponents of *French in Action* claim that this method gives us 'the advantages of immersion without the chaos' (*FIA*: 2). In other words, through video and audio tapes we are given native speakers, using authentic speech in authentic situations. Indeed, the first few lessons, which are given almost entirely in French, 'plunge' the student into far more French than she can hope to understand. The student will then, 'little by little', develop enough knowledge of the language to the point where she expands upon that knowledge 'exponentially'. The programme can be self-taught, or can quite comfortably be used in adult introductory French courses, suggesting that the student who follows the programme to the end (through 52 lessons) will be at approximately intermediate level French.

The most portable aspect of this programme is the framework in which the lessons operate. Like TV Ontario's popular series for ESL, *How Do You Do?*, each *French In Action* lesson concentrates on a specific, functional theme. Such universal second language subjects as families, vacations, food, transportation and living space are the subjects of the first 25 lessons.

The lessons themselves include a tapescript (in the accompanying textbook), with photographs, jokes and line drawings drawn directly from the accompanying audio/video tape. In fact, listening as well as 'visual' comprehension are required from the earliest lessons. Obviously enough, the lessons increase in difficulty as the student advances through them. The essence of this, for our purposes, is that students who have little or no ability in the target language are taken through the beginner level into intermediate skills *through listening*. And though production of spoken language is not a requirement, most students begin to produce in the early lessons. They feel that the early listening period has allowed them to 'internalise' the important suprasegmental features of stress and intonation to the point where they feel comfortable producing the language.

One obvious criticism of this programme is the cost. Students are required to shell out approximately $100.00 Cdn for the textbook, study guide and audio tapes. The video tapes are available for approximately $300.00 Cdn. (They are, of course, free on public television, or through many public and university libraries.) Also, there seems to be less emphasis on the teacher in the teacher-learner equation. But, while many of us in the profession would see both the cost and the self-directed nature of the programme as drawbacks, students often see those features as highly positive. The cost is approximately the same as a teacher-directed course in adult education programmes; the self-directed experience is often sought out by certain kinds of students.

These drawbacks should not deter instructors from having a serious look at the techniques employed by *French in Action*. Moreover, teachers can take heart in the fact that most students view the programme as limited to the earliest stages in their language learning experience, one that implies the eventual – if not early – intervention of a bona fide instructor in the equation. In fact, Capretz himself sees his method as something which should be used to *augment* the introductory language course.

Listening (Anne Anderson & Tony Lynch)

So far, we have seen that there are two features which are essential to a listening approach to teaching a second language – commands or the right to operate on aural information through movement; and the importance of an early silent period. But what if, for various reasons, a group of students refuses to accept the idea of moving around in reaction to spoken material, an idea which seems to many to be puerile, but which is essential to the success of Asher's method; or what if students rebel against the idea of a 'silent period', a reaction not uncommon when students are pressed for time, or when they have paid considerable fees for their instruction. Finally, what if a teacher simply doesn't have the technical equipment available required by the Capretz method, which is certainly a problem in most language teaching environments outside of the college or university level.

In the cases cited above, instructors might wish to consider a book published in the Oxford University Press Language Teaching series, Anne Anderson and Tony Lynch's *Listening*. This textbook is set up specifically to involve language teachers in what the authors call a 'task based' approach to understanding the importance of listening comprehension in the overall process of language learning. This comprehensive and useful – though somewhat short – textbook gives a highly practical outline of listening comprehension. It begins with a research-based perspective which leads into practical suggestions for classroom procedures. Like all other textbooks in OUP's Scheme for Teacher Education series, edited by Chris Candlin and Henry Widdowson, this text includes a section on 'small scale research' projects which teachers might undertake. Although the book does not actually set out a day-to-day syllabus *per se*, it offers the teacher more than a hundred 'tasks' to be employed in various situations in the language class devoted primarily to listening comprehension. As well, language teachers will enjoy the highly readable and, for the most part, non-technical approach taken by Anderson and Lynch.

As noted, slightly over one-third of the book is devoted to research into listening. Teachers are given a working definition of listening comprehension, after which there is extensive discussion of the connection between listening and speaking, and listening and reading. This is followed by a discussion of research into first and second language comprehension. This section of the text is completed by an examination of input, though not, specifically speaking, focusing on Krashen's (1985) model.

While many teachers immediately rebel at the idea of a lengthy research-based discussion in a textbook which is for use in the classroom, the research background in *Listening* is essential. In the first instance, teachers need to understand that listening has normally been relegated to an unimportant place in second language curricula simply because it has not normally been seen as a separate *skill* which can be taught as such. Secondly, instructors must be made aware, from the beginning, that a great deal of practical information can be gleaned from work and observations done in first language listening, practical information which many of us have access to simply because we have often observed children using language. *Listening* makes a strong case for understanding the research which informs task-based teaching of comprehension by setting out more than 50 'tasks' which, on the one hand illustrate important practical uses of the research, and on the other hand, offer a framework into which the classroom practitioner can plug her syllabus.

The second and by far the largest section of *Listening* is devoted to the creation and use of listening materials for the classroom teacher. As well, there are substantial sections on grading, complexity and general evaluation of listening materials. In fact, this section ends with a number of samples from a listening programme, suggesting precisely how the teacher can set up a syllabus for listening using materials which are graded for their complexity from simple to abstract.

The likeliest criticism which teachers might make of this text is that, unlike Asher's and Capretz' methods, this doesn't set out a day-to-day syllabus which the teacher simply needs to follow. However, many would argue that, for listening comprehension in particular, teacher developed materials are essential in second language classrooms because of the need to use as wide a variety of informants as possible. In fact, as we shall see below, it is often unwise to incorporate too many 'canned' listening comprehension materials into the syllabus because they often lack authenticity, an essential element in developing 'native-like' listening comprehension.

The goal in the final section of this chapter is to put the various textbook methods into the light of an actual ESL programme. We shall observe that the relatively stable environment of theories and textbook methods often become the strangest bedfellows when placed into the high relief of daily language classrooms.

Classroom Strategies

Each of (what must loosely be called) the methods noted above is available to the classroom teacher for, in the first and third instances, the normal cost of a textbook, and in the second instance, the cost of study materials and audio tapes. To varying degrees, each requires the intervention of a well-trained classroom teacher of second language, but each has certain problems in its actual 'real world' language teaching implementation.

In this section, I wish to concentrate on classroom strategies for listening comprehension which are employed at the beginner level of a typical second language programme for adolescent and adult learners. From an introductory intensive ESL syllabus, we will observe the objectives, the evaluation techniques for listening comprehension, and the overall approach of second language teachers who have been trained to teach listening comprehension in a teacher-training programme which is based, to a certain extent, on the three methods discussed above.

Level 1 Intensive English for ESL

Textbook: *Speak Up* (Cheryl Pavlik); Video Series: *How Do You Do?* (Part 1)

Objectives: To introduce stress and intonation patterns, and pronunciation of basic English structures, through the the use of elementary vocabulary, audio-visual materials, oral and (occasionally) written exercises. Most material will involve *static* input with a high degree of *explicitness* and *redundancy*, thus ensuring that students are exposed to quasi-authentic listening situations. The goal is to increase confidence while offering considerable advancement to the student's listening skills.

Grading: Progress, 10%; Tests, 15%: Comprehension Exercises, 25%; Pronunciation Exercises, 15%; Listening Comprehension Exams, 35%

Weekly Plan:

Mondays: Listening exercises involving suprasegmental (prosodic) features of sound in English. Frequent use of music.

Tuesdays: First part of *How Do You Do* tape, with emphasis on listening comprehension.

Wednesdays: Approximately three units from *Speak Up*, listening comprehension exercises which involve segmental sound discrimination.

Thursdays: Second part of *How Do You Do* tape, with emphasis on listening comprehension.

Fridays: Evaluation of various structures covered in the three different kinds of listening exercises performed from Monday to Thursday. Tests, Exams and or spontaneous evaluations where possible or necessary.

(After DALS, IELP I Syllabus)

Figure 1.1 Example Syllabus

Figure 1.1 is the overview of a one-page course outline usually given out to teachers in the Intensive ESL programme at Brock University's Department of Applied Language Studies. From this, we gain insight into the processes normally followed by teachers of second language comprehension. This is the typical shell syllabus given to teachers of a 'false beginners' course in second language comprehension for intensive ESL. The teacher is then expected to submit, on a weekly basis, a class activity sheet for the five one-hour classes to take place during the week. The one-hour class for listening is one of five hours of study during each day. The duration of the course is approximately 14 weeks, or the approximate equivalent of one academic term. There is a certain amount of coordination between the listening comprehension and speaking courses at this level, but the teacher is expected to concentrate on listening for at least the one hour devoted to that particular skill.

Through a cursory examination of the syllabus, it should be immediately evident that the laudable goals of developing listening comprehension through movement, the right to delayed oral production, and even the task-based orientation to listening comprehension, are not always easy to introduce and employ, even in what must certainly be considered an optimum environment. In fact, it is clear to applied linguists and practitioners alike that methods employed successfully in the laboratory environment of teacher training – through peer teaching, observation and actual in-class practice – are hard-won at best, or simply impractical at worst in the 'real-world' second language classroom. Though this is sometimes discouraging to the applied linguist, the inventiveness and practicality of teachers in adapting themselves to the world beyond the teacher training environment ought to be heartening to the seasoned teacher.

As we can see, a great deal of the course is devoted to listening comprehension. However, a specific feature of this course is the emphasis on prosodic as well as segmental features of sound. In fact, students in this course frequently begin work on prosodic features without recourse to segmental sound. In other words, they focus on the stress and intonation patterns of English without the interference of segments (i.e. the phonemes that make up words, etc.) in order to concentrate on the difficult problem of 'accent'.

With the use of audio tapes that accompany *Speak Up*, and video tapes for the *How Do You Do?* series, the beginning student is also exposed to a great many speakers of English, something which is afforded in this programme because students focus on the reading, writing and speaking skills in three other hours of study throughout the school day. As well, students are not *required* to produce oral responses to the listening comprehension material until they feel comfortable doing so. This would certainly fit well within the purposes outlined above in the discussion of Asher and Capretz: however, we at Brock's Intensive ESL Program have discovered that most students are keen to *produce* English and seem generally unwilling to 'delay' their production very long.

The question of evaluation poses the most serious difficulties at this stage in listening comprehension. If we were to follow Asher's lead, we would employ commands and movement as such an approach to evaluation would certainly take the stress out of the equation for the student. But we have discovered its impracticalities, one of which is that movement in response to commands is virtually impossible to standardise for evaluation purposes, and students do require some form of stand-ardised evaluation. For that reason, we tend to combine a limited amount of the movement and command style evaluation with the more traditional 'dictation' or 'circling the correct response' test. We also employ cloze exercises, along with the others. While we have found such forms of evaluation to be acceptable to the students, we are troubled enough by the 'skill gap' between listening comprehension and these 'writing-based' evaluation techniques that we are working on methods that employ speaking and even gestural and other paralinguistic responses.

All of which of course brings us almost back to where we started – listening as a skill-based part of the second language curriculum. As is obvious from the example syllabus above, listening has come into its own as a recognised and separate skill to be taught as such in the language teaching environment. And though listening comprehension is no longer relegated to the drudgery of cassette tapes in the language lab, or *dictées* in the classroom, its successful evaluation seems doomed to employ, to at least some extent, the skill of writing, while its successful implementation requires access to some form of audio or audiovisual reproduction. Perhaps we should be pleased with the developments thus far. But we should also be determined to eventually employ, almost uniquely, an extensive range of listening oriented techniques and methods in this, the first language skill.

References

Anderson, A. and Lynch, T. (1988) *Listening*. Oxford: Oxford University Press.
Asher, J. (1977) *Learning Another Language Through Actions: The Complete Teacher's Guidebook*. Los Gatos: Sky Oaks Productions.
Capretz, P. (1987) *French In Action*. New Haven: Yale University Press.

Courchêne, R.J., Glidden, J.I., St John, J. and Thérien, C. (eds) (1992) *Comprehension Based Second Language Teaching*. Ottawa: University of Ottawa Press.

Glissan, E. (1993) Total physical response: A technique for teaching all skills in Spanish. In J. Oller (ed.) *Methods that Work: Ideas for Literacy and Language Teachers* (pp. 30–39). Boston: Heinle and Heinle.

Gregg, K. (1984) Krashen's monitor and Occam's razor. *Applied Linguistics* 5 (2).

Hammerly, H. (1989) French immersion: Does it work? *CMLR* 45 (3).

Irons, G. and Paribakht, S. (1992) *Make Changes Make a Difference*. Welland, Ontario: Editions Soleil.

Krashen, S. (1985) *The Input Hypothesis*. Oxford: Pergamon.

Krashen, S. and Terrell, T. (1983) *The Natural Approach*. Oxford: Pergamon.

Pavlik, C. (1985) *Speak Up: Beginning Pronunciation and Task Listening*. New York: Newbury House

Terrell, T. and Krashen, S. (1983) *The Natural Approach*. Oxford: Pergamon.

Gladstone, J. *How Do You Do? Viewer's Guide A and B*. Toronto: Fitzhenry and Whiteside (in association with TV Ontario).

Winitz, H. (1981) *The Comprehension Approach to Foreign Language Instruction*. Rowley, MA: Newbury House.

2 Increasing Comprehension Skills Through Listening and Asking Questions

ANNE BOURQUE and SYLVAIN JACQUES

The use of a variety of questioning techniques by both teachers and students will be examined, with suggested strategies to promote increased oral communication, develop better listening skills and a higher level of critical thinking and comprehension through self-discovery and teacher-directed strategies. Making communication in a second language more accessible to second language learners is the focus of an interactive communicative language environment where the stimuli are using the new language in a meaningful context, as a realistic tool, in an effort to motivate students to broaden their vocabulary and comprehension skills.

Introduction

Language instruction which is grounded in derivation and communication of meaning is a holistic and high level concept. In order for students to learn language, they must, from the beginning, be engaged in making sense of the language and in composing and communicating meaning. When language learning shifts from a focus on structures to a focus on meaning, a paradox occurs. The derivation, composition and communication of meaning become simultaneously the goals of second language learning and the strategies which enable students to achieve that learning.

The choice of appropriate contexts for learning and the attention to the quality of student engagement are the new basics. Meaning can only be explored in a context which is meaningful to the learner and it is only in such a context that the reason to know and the need to communicate will be perceived as genuine. The making of meaning will only occur to the extent to which learners are actively engaged. Especially in a second language arena, with its direct focus on meaning, students must be involved in their own learning. They must not only investigate, explore and complete projects, but also discover meaning, process information and experiences, solve problems and integrate knowledge in a way that makes sense to them.

Performance Objectives

Students will be able to:

(1) Actively use questioning techniques to stimulate learning and meaning in a second language.
(2) Orally use and reinforce new vocabulary and structures in a context of questions and answers.
(3) Listen to key words as clues to an overall meaning.
(4) Actively participate in short, contextualised conversations that will promote self-discovery and feelings of adequacy towards a new language.

Language teachers who deal with learners being exposed to a second language for the first time understand the importance of developing comprehension skills through listening and asking questions. Questioning, a process of guided learning, is one of the most important teaching strategies we employ. Skilful questioning can:

- Establish and maintain student listening skills
- Help build a positive learning tone in the classroom
- Extend creative thinking
- Improve problem solving processing
- Build students self-concept
- Increase social learning
- Improve academic results

The following implementation strategies must be seen in the context of a total, holistic, integrated and communicative language programme. The key to student engagement lies in providing students with materials which are authentic, contexts which are relevant, and learning experiences which are appropriate to their age, intellectual and interest levels. In doing so, we provide the learner with the optimum environment in which to experience real meaning in all its complexity and to participate actively and creatively in the language learning process; for the making of meaning is the result of the dynamic interplay of a large number of factors, some which can be directly taught, and some which rely on the individual's unique and personal insights and interpretations.

Learning and Teaching Strategies

The strategies suggested here are designed to help create an environment in which language is experienced holistically and personally respects the integrity of the language as well as that of the learner.

Listening to the music

WHY? To promote listening skills with authentic musical representation.

HOW? (1) Teacher selects a piece of music related to a theme/unit (based on the age level, interests, and comprehension level of students).

(2) While listening to the selected piece of music, students complete the following questionnaire.

(3) Once completed, students can share their answers, perceptions, and preferences with the group as a whole or within small groups. (Refer to Appendix 2.1.)

Likes and dislikes

WHY? To provide the opportunity for students to exchange personal information with brief and simple oral messages, sharing likes/dislikes, interests, and using phrases and expressions which are useful in many different situations.

To allow students to experiment with questioning in one-on-one interactions.

HOW? (1) Students complete a chart individually (Refer to Appendix 2.2.)

(2) Students are then paired so that they can find out about their partner through the use of various types of questions.
Example: Tu aimes écouter la musique classique?
(You like to listen to classical music?)
Est-ce que tu aimes regarder le hockey?
(Are you a hockey fan?)
Qu'est-ce que tu aimes faire?
(What do you like to do?)
Aimes-tu manger le sushi?
(Do you like to eat sushi?)

This activity would require, as a prerequisite, an introduction to the ways of asking questions (inversion, est-ce que... and intonation). The vocabulary building potential of this activity is limitless and would allow students to discover new vocabulary on their own. More personalised and perhaps better retention would be the reward.

Split images

WHY? To help students evoke mental images.

HOW? Students, working with partners, are named partner A and partner B. 'A' looks at a picture being held up by the teacher and describes what they see to partner 'B'. On a signal, Bs look up as the teacher holds a second picture and they describe what they see to partner A. This continues until all illustrations for an unfamiliar story have been shown. After seeing the illustrations, partners predict what the story is going to be about. Predictions are presented to the class by partners, the story could be told as a prediction circle story, or a variety of activities could take place. Then the partners are given the story as the author wrote it to read together.

Example of stories:

The teacher could start with a familiar story (e.g. a fairytale (*Cinderella*), a legend, (*Big Foot*) and could gradually move to a story the students are not familiar with, therefore using base knowledge to extend their use of questioning and descriptive language. In this activity, students would have the opportunity to ask questions or describe events simply by using a picture as a reference. Piecing together orally given information will stimulate a higher level of thinking, sequencing, the use of specific clues, and promote good listening skills.

My secret identity

WHY? To practise the interrogative form of 'Am I... ?'. To promote the development of deductive reasoning/ thinking.

HOW? (1) Prepare adhesive labels (file folder labels) with the names of famous people from different backgrounds (authors, musicians, politicians, actors, singers, athletes, etc.).

(2) Each student has an adhesive label attached to his back so as not to see who he/she is representing.

(3) Form groups of four to six students.

(4) In each group, each student has the chance to ask questions (to discover his identity) after having identified himself to the rest of the group. The student then asks questions to that end.

Example: Est-ce que je suis un homme? (Am I a man?)
Est-ce que je suis une femme? (Am I a woman?)
Est-ce que je suis canadien? (Am I a Canadian?)
Est-ce que je suis vivant... mort... jeune... vieux, etc.
(Am I living?... dead?... young?... old?... etc.).

(5)   This process continues until all the members of the group
      have discovered their secret identity.

Crystal ball

WHY?   To predict the outcome of a story before reading it.

       To expand upon students vocabulary through the use of key
       words.

       To allow students to make inferences.

HOW?   (1)   Choose 20 words found in a story to be read later.

       (2)   Divide students into groups of four.

       (3)   Each group receives the list of 20 words and must create a
             story incorporating the selected words along with additional
             words.

       (4)   Each team then shares their version of the story to the class.

       (5)   Read the actual story and see what group came closest to
             predicting the true outcome of the story.

The teacher could begin this activity with a story that is familiar to the
students (as a practice exercise) and then move on to an unfamiliar story as
the students better understand the activity.

For example:

slipper	mice	dress	lose
god-mother	poor	a ball	run
step-mother	beautiful	midnight	love
prince	sisters	work	handsone
chariot	girl	evil	

Answer: *Cinderella*
(Brownlie *et al.*, 1992).

Brainstorm and classification

WHY? To increase students' vocabulary in certain theme areas (e.g. sports, clothing, food, transportation, etc.).

To promote cooperative learning groups and decision-making.

HOW? (1) Brainstorm with the whole class to bring out vocabulary from the specific theme (example: name all the sports you can think of in the target language).

(2) List all student responses on the blackboard.

(3) Students are then paired and receive a chart on which they must classify the vocabulary in specific categories (example: team sports, individual sports, winter sports, indoor sports, etc.).

(4) At the end of the exercise, each pair must invent two new categories that have not been included on the original chart (example: sports played with a ball, sports using rackets, violent sports, sports requiring special equipment, etc.).

Story pyramid

WHY? To provide students with a framework in order to identify principal characters, situations, problems, main events and solutions to a story.

To help students better express their ideas using a limited number of words.

To improve listening skills using the key elements of a story.

HOW? (1) After reading a story to the students, they summarise the events of the story using the following clues.

1st line: the name of the main character.

2nd line: two words that describe the main character.

3rd line: three words that describe the location of the story.

4th line: four words that explain the problem.

5th line: five words that describe the first important event in the story.

6th line: six words that describe a second important event.

7th line: seven words that describe a third important event.

8th line: eight words that describe the solution or the outcome of the story.

Example:

                                                                    1. _____

                                                          2. _____ _____

                                              3. _____ _____ _____

                                  4. _____ _____ _____ _____

                      5. _____ _____ _____ _____ _____

          6. _____ _____ _____ _____ _____ _____

      7. _____ _____ _____ _____ _____ _____ _____

8. _____ _____ _____ _____ _____ _____ _____ _____

Guided visualisation

WHY?   To stimulate students' imagination prior to completing a writing activity.

To exercise students' listening skills.

HOW? (1)   Students close their eyes and concentrate.

(2)   The teacher reads a text or asks questions that will permit students to visualise images (special places, people, things, etc).

(3)   The students note what they see as the teacher reads the text or asks the questions after setting the stage for the visualisation. For example, Que vois-tu? Qui est là? Que font-ils? Que fais-tu?

(4)   Students could also illustrate what they imagined and then, depending on language ability, they could share the images they saw during the visualisation exercise within small groups or with the class as a whole.

The chosen text in this case would have to reflect the knowledge (i.e. vocabulary, structures, etc.) already introduced to the students. It would act as a reinforcement of new material and would also help students to piece together the newly acquired vocabulary in a new setting and under new circumstances, thus having them discover meaning.

The overall goal has been and continues to be that of helping students learn how to ask questions, seek answers or solutions to satisfy their curiosity, and to build their own theories and ideas about the world.

Getting students to think, solve problems, and discover things for themselves are not new goals in education. However, we have to emphasise the importance of discovery learning and how teachers can help learners become 'constructionists' or builders of their own knowledge.

Appendix 2.1

Écoutez la musique...

(1) Est-ce que c'est de la musique?
     (Is this music?)

<table>
<tr><td></td><td>rap</td></tr>
<tr><td>FOLKLORIQUE</td><td>rock'n roll</td></tr>
<tr><td>Instrumentale</td><td></td></tr>
<tr><td></td><td>classique</td></tr>
</table>

(2) Est-ce que la personne qui chante est un/e...
     (Is the person who is singing a...)

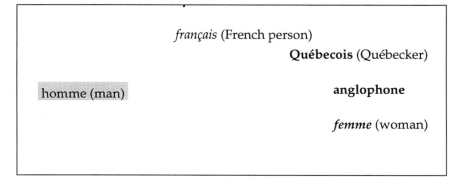

français (French person)

Québecois (Québecker)

homme (man)

anglophone

femme (woman)

(3) Je comprends ces mots…
(I understand these words…)

_____   _____   _____

_____   _____   _____

_____   _____   _____

(4) Il s'agit de…
(This is…)

_____

_____

Appendix 2.2

LES CHOSES QUE J'AIME ET QUE JE N'AIME PAS

J'aime écouter… (I like to listen to…)	Je n'aime pas écouter… (I do not like to listen to…)
J'aime faire… (I like to do…)	Je n'aime pas faire… (I do not like to do…)
J'aime manger… (I like to eat…)	Je n'aime pas manger… (I do not like to eat…)
J'aime regarder… (I like to watch..)	Je n'aime pas regarder… (I do not like to watch…)
J'aime sentir… (I like to smell…)	Je n'aime pas sentir… (I do not like to smell…)

References

Bellanca, J. and Fogarty, R. (1986) *Catch them Thinking*. Illinois: Skylight.
— (1990) *Blueprints for Thinking in the Cooperative Classroom*. Illinois: Skylight.
Bellavance, R. (1991) L'enseignant face à l'erreur. *Le journal de l'immersion*, 15 (1), 29–33.
Besse, H. (1987) Enseigner la compétence de communication? In P. Calvé and A. Mollica (eds) *Le Français langue seconde: des principes à la pratique* (pp. 173–82). Welland: La Revue canadienne des langues vivantes.
Brownlie, F., Close, S. and Wingren, L. (1988) *Reaching for Higher Thought: Reading, Writing, Thinking Strategies*. Edmonton, Alberta: Arnold Publishing.
— (1989) *Tomorrow's Classroom Today: Strategies for Creating Active Readers, Writers and Thinkers*. Markham, Ontario: Pembroke Publishers.

— (1992) *Beyond Chalk and Talk: Collaborative Strategies for the Middle to High School Years*. Markham, Ontario: Pembroke Publishers.

Calvé, P. (1987) Les programmes de base: des principes à la réalité. In P. Calvé and A. Mollica (eds) *Le Français langue seconde: des principes à la pratique* (pp. 16–32). Welland, Ontario: La Revue canadienne des langues vivantes.

Holdaway, D. (1984) *Stability and Change in Literacy Learning*. Portsmouth, NH: Heinemann.

Johnson, D.W. (1990) *Cooperation in the Classroom*. Edina, MN: Interaction Book Company.

Ministry of Education (Curriculum Development Branch) (1991) *Decision-making in Literature: Enhancing and Evaluating Oral Communication in the Primary Grades*. Victoria, BC.

— (Curriculum Development Branch) (1991) *Learning Through Reading: Teaching Strategies Resource Book*. Victoria, BC.

— (Curriculum Development Branch) (1991) *Programme du primaire: document de base*. Victoria, BC.

Rowe, M.B. (1986) Wait time: Slowing down may be a way of speeding up. *Journal of Teacher Education* 37, 43–50.

Stern, H.H. (1987) Les programmes de français de base au Canada: comment les améliorer? In P. Calvé and A. Mollica (eds) *Le Français langue seconde: des principes la pratique* (pp. 1–15). Welland, Ontario: La Revue canadienne des langues vivantes.

Stevens, R. (1912) The question as a measure of efficiency in instruction: A critical study of classroom practice. In *Teachers College Contributions to Education* 48. NY: Teachers College Press.

Stipek, D.J. (1988) *Motivation to Learn: From Theory to Practice*. Englewood Cliffs, NJ: Prentice-Hall.

Tompkins, G.E. and Hoskisson, K. (1991) *Language Arts: Content and Teaching Strategies*. NY: Merrill.

Tremblay, R., Painchaud, G., Leblanc, R. and Comeau, M. (1989) *Se lancer en affaires avec un jeu*. Winnipeg, Manitoba: Association canadienne des professeurs de langue seconde.

Weiss, F. (1987) Types de communication et activités communicatives en classe. In P. Calvé and A. Mollica (eds). *Le Français langue seconde: des principes à la pratique* (pp. 190–7). Welland, Ontario: La Revue canadienne des langues vivantes.

Widdowson, H.G. (1978) *Teaching Language as Communication*. London: Oxford University Press.

Wisconsin Department of Public Instruction (1991) *Strategic Learning in the Content Areas*. Wisconsin.

3 Teaching the Receptive Skills at the Basic Level

GISÈLE PAINCHAUD and RAYMOND LEBLANC

Receptive skills, long thought to be an offshoot of production, are now being recognised as an integral part of any language teaching/learning approach. But while this long-overdue recognition is happening, a number of questions remain as to the teachability of these skills. This chapter first examines the theoretical foundations of receptive skills teaching/learning. Then, drawing on seven years of receptive skills teaching at the University of Ottawa, the authors show how, given a definite set of performance objectives, these can be attained in the classroom through the proper teaching strategy.

Communication through language implies the successful transmission of a spoken or written message. For this transmission to occur, a minimum of two basic conditions must be met: (1) senders must be able to encode their message in such a way that it says what they want it to say; and (2) receivers must be able to decode it. There are thus two obvious sets of skills needed for communication to be successful: the productive skills (encoding) and the receptive skills (decoding). The complementarity of these two skills is but common sense and is accepted by all. However, when it comes to teaching them, things do not seem to be so clear.

In fact, second language teaching lore says that the receptive skills, while essential to communication, can be acquired through the teaching of the productive skills. This is certainly true in the writings of highly celebrated authors:

It seems important to recognize the fact that one's mastery of any language – even of one's own native language – is always on two major levels, *production* and *recognition*. [...] This recognition of the difference between the production and the receptive controls of language does not imply a mechanical separation of the materials into 'practices' for producing for the sake of production only and 'practices' in recognition for the sake of receiving only. As a matter of fact *practice in production is one of the best means of developing recognition*. (Fries, 1945: 8 – our italics)

It is also true in the practice of language teaching as illustrated by materials in use in the second or foreign language classrooms to this day where the accent is squarely put on production from the very start and where only lip service (pardon the pun!) is paid to the receptive skills.

But with the emphasis now put on communication (as opposed to form), the shortcomings of the traditional production-based approach are becoming more and more apparent and the need for a broader approach to language teaching that will take into account at least the main components of communication is obvious. An important aspect of this broader approach must be the development of the learner's receptive skills. In the following pages, we would first like to discuss the basis for the inclusion of the receptive skills in the curriculum, then, after presenting the types of performance objectives that can be reached by learners at the basic level, show how these can be achieved through the use of *ad hoc* strategies.

The Receptive Skills in the Curriculum

Although language teaching through some form of comprehension-based approach is very recent in terms of the history of language teaching, it has already produced a significant number of movements. These include, among others, the Total Physical Response approach, the immersion programmes, the Natural Approach and the content-based courses.

During the 1960s, two highly significant receptive-skill oriented approaches were introduced. In the early part of the decade, a systematic comprehension-based approach was first advocated by Asher (1965, 1969, 1977). He named his approach the Total Physical Response (TPR). In this approach, students are asked to show their understanding of sets of directions by actually performing them. In other words, students listen and react, as would happen in the normal use of the language. These directions can range from simple orders in the imperative to much more complex directions, involving conditions, for instance. Although limited in scope to concrete language, TPR has had and continues to have a large following, especially for beginner level language teaching.

At about the same time, in 1965, the first immersion programme was being set up in St. Lambert, in the Province of Quebec (Lambert & Tucker, 1972). Stern (1984) describes immersion as a programme of studies where subject matters (mathematics, history, arts, physical education, etc.) are taught in the second language. The objective is to promote the acquisition of the target language through other disciplines as opposed to the regular second language course. It is then a situation where students are asked to listen (and read, later on) and are expected to perform on that basis.

Immersion programmes, for all their flaws, have been an enormous success and have clearly shown that learning of both subject matter content and of the target language does occur through such an approach (LeBlanc, 1992).

In the 1970s, Postovsky (1972, 1974) , Winitz and Reeds (1973), and Nord (1978) showed by their research results that significant gains could be made in the actual learning of a second or foreign language by delaying the introduction of the production component of that language.

It is, however, from the 1980s on that research and practice in the teaching of the receptive skills came to the fore. The impulse given by Krashen's (1982, 1985) *Input Hypothesis*, Long's (1983, 1985) *Interactional Hypothesis* as well as Smith's (1982) work on reading, led to a number of significant contributions to this new field. Byrnes (1984), Faerch and Kasper (1986), and Morley (1984) on the role of listening comprehension in second language learning; Oxford (1985, 1990) and O'Malley *et al.* (1989) on the place of strategies; Brown (1977, 1986) and Kramsch (1992) on the influence of context; Carrell (1983, 1984) on schema, together with other contributions such as Chaudron (1985), Ellis (1985, 1992), Richards (1983) and Courchêne *et al.* (1992), to name but a few, gave this aspect of second language teaching the needed foundations on which to build.

As is normal, the practice of receptive skills teaching took some time to catch on. Of note, however, are the early contributions of Krashen and Terrell (1983), *The Natural Approach*, developed taking into account Krashen's views on language acquisition noted earlier, as well as the Content-Based Approach where students are taught the target subject matter in their second language and receive coaching from a language teacher to help them with whatever difficulties they might encounter (Edwards *et al.*, 1984, Hauptman *et al.*, 1989).

One of the most extensive applications of the receptive skills approach is that currently in use at the University of Ottawa. Because this university is bilingual, all its students must meet some form of second language requirement before graduation. In 1986, it was decided that the L2 requirements for the students of its two largest faculties would be defined in terms of receptive skills only. This translates into some 1,500 students taking comprehension-based courses from the beginning to the intermediate level. For details on this and the early approach used, see LeBlanc (1986). Of course, this situation created conditions where expertise was needed at both the conceptual and the application levels. Progressively, materials were designed, classroom practices were tested and evaluation procedures were developed, with the result that in 1990, an international symposium was organised by the Second Language Institute of the University of

Ottawa which brought together a number of specialists from Canada and abroad and culminated with the publication of a major work on the topic (Courchêne *et al.*, 1992). The next two sections of this chapter will draw mostly from the experience in comprehension-based language teaching at the University of Ottawa.

The Performance Objectives

Contrary to speaking, for instance, where the satisfactory production of a target sound, word, sentence, or exchange will demonstrate some level of learning and prove to the students' satisfaction that they are making progress, the acquisition of the receptive skills is much less obvious and clear performance objectives must be defined if students (and teacher) are to be aware that they are indeed improving their second language ability. The question then becomes: Can listening and reading be broken down into teachable and learnable units or are these two skills essentially global in nature? To answer, one must examine some of the characteristics of these skills.

Four categories of objectives

Understanding a spoken or a written message first requires a certain level of linguistic ability. In fact, the more sophisticated the intended level of understanding, the better the knowledge of the linguistic code must become (Painchaud, 1990). This implies, not surprisingly, language objectives. It must be remembered, however, that the basic unit of communication goes well beyond the sentence level and that language objectives must include some level of mastery of discourse as well as the more traditional sound, grammar and vocabulary.

But the ability to understand a spoken or a written text implies more than some level of linguistic competence. In any communication attempt, the speaker/writer and the listener/reader are deemed to share a certain level of common knowledge, practices, beliefs, values, and so on, which underlie the message and are essential to its correct interpretation. The speaker/writer obviously shares part of the responsibility for this but a similar contribution is expected from the listener/reader. This implies some level of cultural knowledge and experience (LeBlanc *et al.*, 1990) and must also be part of the objectives of any comprehension-based course.

Research on the competent listener/reader has also shown the importance of being able to use general knowledge on language and culture as well as appropriate strategies when trying to understand a text. It stands to reason that students lacking in communicative competence and attempting to deal with complex situations will gain by using everything at their disposal to help them perform the task at hand. This is what Hébert (1990) calls 'general language education' and it should be part of any set of objectives in comprehension.

It must be remembered, though, that these three sets of objectives (language, culture, and general language education), important as they are, will not by themselves be sufficient to render language learners able to use their receptive skills communicatively. Learning to communicate requires both the relevant knowledge and practice in communication. It is thus fundamental that the language curriculum contain objectives of a communicative nature. Tremblay *et al.* (1990) and LeBlanc (1990) believe that these objectives should be experiential in nature, that is, they should make use of students' life experiences as the contexts in which to set meaningful communicative efforts.

Some performance objectives

A *general objective* for a basic level comprehension-based course could be as follows:

Students will be able to understand relevant spoken and written texts at the level of the identification of the topic and of factual contents and to formulate simple hypotheses based on these contents.

The level of comprehension chosen for these students is in line with the mental processes progression as established by Courchêne (1992) where he shows it to increase in complexity as follows: Recognition and recall → Inferring equivalences → Evaluative synthetic reasoning → Judgemental, critical thinking (p. 106).

To demonstrate that they have reached this general objective, students must show an acceptable level of ability in a set of 'performance objectives'. Because this is written without a specific curriculum in mind, a large number of performance objectives could be relevant for students working on their receptive skills at the basic level; but choices have to be made for this text to remain within the predetermined length parameters. The first of such choices is to deal with reading, more specifically with understanding written instructions.

In accordance with our earlier discussion, reading performance objectives must fall under four categories.

(1) **Communicative/experiential objectives**
   (a) Students will be able to act upon a set of instructions with precision.
   (b) Students will be able to compare their new knowledge with their previous experience in the area of the chosen text.
(2) **Language objectives**
   (c) Students will be able to identify the markers of instructions written in the imperative.
   (d) Students will be able to identify temporal and conditional circumstances signalled by 'quand' (when) and 'si' (if).
(3) **Culture objectives**
   (e) Students will be able to draw conclusions from a comparison of instructions in L2 with instructions in L1 in a similar context.
   (f) Students will show they have learned cultural facts by using them correctly in the chosen context.
(4) **General language education objectives**
   (g) Students will use their L1 knowledge in understanding an L2 text.
   (h) Students will use their C1 (cultural) knowledge in understanding an L2 text.
   (i) Students will use inference as a means to understanding an L2 text.

As should be obvious, other and more numerous performance objectives could have been selected. These should prove useful, however, to illustrate what can actually be done in the comprehension-based classroom.

Teaching the Receptive Skills

According to Tremblay *et al.* (1990), a communicative/experiential activity should lead to a concrete observable end-product. For this presentation, we have chosen to illustrate a situation where our university students have heard about a new game on the market (for instance *Le docte rat*) and are interested in playing it. The written text to be understood (to which the teaching approach will be applied) is that of the rules of the game and the observable end-product is being able to play the game according to the rules (obj. a). And since, in this case, being able to play correctly implies knowledge of culture related facts, these will be deemed known when the end-product is reached (obj. f).

Authors agree that in oral or written text presentations, a three-step sequence (Pre-activity, Activity, Post-activity) should be followed (Duplantie and Massey 1984; LeBlanc 1986; Tremblay *et al.* 1990, among others). Let us illustrate how this could be applied to our chosen situation.

Pre-activity

Teachers should always prepare their students to hear or read a text. This is because the comprehension of a text is strongly linked to the hypotheses the listener/reader makes about it. It should be obvious that to understand a text, one must have some relevant knowledge about its content. This knowledge is presumed by the speaker/writer in the case of L1. Such cannot be the case where the L2 students are concerned. The pre-activity step is aimed at closing the gaps that might exist among students and at establishing the context of the text.

The pre-activity should include the contextualisation of the text. In our example, this could lead to questions such as: Are you familiar with games? Have you played any? Which ones have you heard about? What is your favourite game? Why? Beginning students will obviously have to answer such questions in their L1. This is totally acceptable since the aim of the exercise is to establish context. It also shows students the relevance of the topic for them (general obj.).

The second phase of the pre-activity should be the anticipation of content and form (obj. i). Again L1 will be used and again this is correct. For the students' contribution to be built upon later on, the teacher should note them on the board using only the target language. This ensures input from students and a first contact with the possible lexicon and phrases of the day's topic.

Activity

With students now at ease with the topic, it is time to go to the activity proper. There are many different ways to do this. One of them could be as follows. At first reading, students are asked to underline the words they think they recognise. At first, students are not very good at this but once they understand that what is expected of them is that they use their L1 knowledge, they become very good at using this strategy (obj. g). Of course this will lead to some errors (the French preposition 'car' mistaken for the English noun 'car') but these mistakes can be used to do some remedial work if warranted and, by and large, the strategy is much more often useful than harmful. Once the underlined words have been shared, students can be asked to try to guess the meaning of the word next to the underlined one. Because words tend to appear in pre-set clusters in all languages, this can lead to the discovery of some of the L2 phrases on the topic (obj. g).

Students can then be asked to read the text a second time, paying attention to its structure (general aim of the game, what is needed to play, how to begin, what happens if… , what happens when… , how to keep score, how to determine a winner, etc.). These are facts that can be found in the text (general obj.) and, in this instance, students are likely to find that their knowledge about L1 games of the same type is proving very useful in their understanding of the L2 text (obj. h).

Armed with their new lexical and organisational knowledge and with the realisation that their L1 knowledge can be most useful, students should be ready for a last pass at the text. This time, they will be asked to make educated guesses at those passages that remain obscure (What would be the logical thing to appear now? What would you have written now?) (obj. i).

Post-activity

The post-activity phase is where teacher and students reflect on what has been happening so far and where students are given the opportunity to hone the abilities put to the fore through the text. First, the teacher should make use of the hypotheses on content and form made by students in the pre-activity phase. This will add value to the pre-activity as students will have an opportunity to compare their expectations with the actual text content. It will also allow them to see what part of their previous experiences helped them and what new knowledge on game rules they have acquired through working on this text (obj. b).

The teacher could then lead a discussion where the rules of the L2 game are compared with those of a selection of L1 games. Is the format the same? Are rules couched in the same terms? If there are significant differences, why is it so? It may happen that there is no difference in the way things are organised in both cultures; the opposite will also happen. In either case, however, the objective of reflecting on the ways of the other culture remains a valid one (obj. e).

The post-activity phase is also the one where linguistic knowledge and ability are most likely to be featured. For instance, in the rules of the game, students will have come across directions given in the imperative. Assuming that this is part of the programme, it would be a most opportune time to show students how this type of instruction is constructed (no subject, imperative morphemes) and to have exercises on this aspect of the language (obj. c). Same thing, *mutatis mutandis*, for the conditional and the temporal circumstances (obj. d). Of course, a number of other linguistic aspects might have been chosen. There should be one guiding principle in that respect: the quantity of linguistic content that can be isolated from a text for systematic study must be directly proportional to the importance of this content for the proper understanding of the text. The only communicatively motivated grammar is the one that is essential (or very useful) to the understanding of the text. The rest becomes grammar for grammar's sake and we should know by now that this is not the approach to use in a communicative setting.

The last step of the post-activity will be the observable output: in our case, actually playing the game. This will allow teachers and students alike to see what was clearly, less clearly and not at all understood (obj. a; obj. f) and can serve as a last chance to formulate hypotheses as to the functioning of the game, a portion of the general objective.

Conclusion

Throughout the chapter, we have tried to show that receptive skills constitute a valid object of instruction and that they can be taught. Because of space limitations, a context had to be created and performance objectives adjusted to it to illustrate how objectives can be transformed into classroom activities. This situation is not altogether so different from the real one in the classroom where students are asked to vote on a selection of texts that will constitute the course content. The teacher then decides what parts of the programme will be covered with each text, making sure that all decisions are communication-based. This is the only way to communicative language teaching.

References

Asher, J.J. (1965) The strategy of the total physical response: An application to learning Russian. *The Modern Language Journal* 3, 44.
— (1969). The total physical response approach to second language learning. *The Modern Language Journal* 53.
— (1977) *Learning Another Language Through Actions*. Los Gatos, CA: Sky Oaks Productions.
Brown, G. (1977) *Listening to Spoken English*. London: Longman.
— (1986) Investigating listening comprehension in context. *Applied Linguistics* 7, 3.
Byrnes, H. (1984) The role of listening comprehension: A theoretical basis. *Foreign Language Annals* 17, 4.
Carrell, P.L. (1983) Three components of background knowledge in reading comprehension. *Language Learning* 33.
— (1984) Evidence of a formal schema in second language comprehension. *Language Learning* 34.
Chaudron, C. (1985) Comprehension, comprehensibility, and learning in the second language classroom. *Studies in Second Language Acquisition* 7.
Courchêne, R. (1992) A comprehension-based approach to curriculum design. In R. Courchêne, J.I. Glidden, J. St John and C. Thérien *Comprehension-based Second*

Language Teaching/L'enseignement des langues secondes axé sur la compréhension.
Ottawa: University of Ottawa Press.

Courchêne, R., Glidden, J.I., St. John, J. and Thérien, C. (1992) *Comprehension-based Second Language Teaching/L'enseignement des langues secondes axé sur la compréhension.* Ottawa: University of Ottawa Press.

Duplantie, M. and Massey, M. (1984) Proposition pour une pédagogie de l'écoute des documents authentiques oraux en classe de langue seconde. *Études de linguistique appliquée* 56.

Edwards, H., Wesche, M., Krashen, S., Clément, R. and Krudenier, B. (1984) Second language acquisition through subject-matter learning: A study of sheltered psychology classes at the University of Ottawa. *Canadian Modern Language Review* 41.

Ellis, R. (1985) *Understanding Second Language Acquisition.* Oxford: Oxford University Press.

— (1992) Comprehension and the acquisition of grammatical knowledge in a second language. In R. Courchêne, J.I. Glidden, J. St. John and C. Thérien (eds) *Comprehension-based Second Language Teaching/L'enseignement des langues secondes axé sur la compréhension.* Ottawa: University of Ottawa Press.

Faerch, C. and Kasper, G. (1986) The role of comprehension in second language learning. *Applied Linguistics* 7.

Fries, C. C. (1945) *Teaching and Learning English as a Foreign Language.* Ann Arbor: University of Michigan Press.

Hauptman, P., Wesche, M. and Ready, D. (1989) Second language acquisition through subject-matter learning: A follow-up study at the University of Ottawa. *Language Learning* 38.

Hébert, Y. (1990) *Étude nationale sur les programmes de français de base: Le syllabus formation langagière générale.* Winnipeg: CASLT & M Éditeur.

Kramsch, C. (1992) Contextes de compréhension. In R. Courchêne, J.I. Glidden, J. St John and C. Thérien (eds) *Comprehension-based Second Language Teaching/L'enseignement des langues secondes axé sur la compréhension.* Ottawa: University of Ottawa Press.

Krashen, S.D. (1982) *Principles and Practice in Second Language Acquisition.* New York: Prentice-Hall.

— (1985) *The Input Hypothesis.* New York: Longman.

Krashen, S. and Terrell, T. (1983) *The Natural Approach: Language Acquisition in the Classroom.* Hayward, CA: Alemany Press.

Lambert, W. and Tucker, R. (1972) *Bilingual Education of Children: The St Lambert Experiment.* Rowley, MA: Newbury House.

LeBlanc, C., Courtel, C. and Trescases, P. (1990) *Étude nationale sur les programmes de français de base: Le syllabus Culture.* Winnipeg: CASLT & M Éditeur.

LeBlanc, R. (1986) L'Écoute dans l'enseignement des langues à des débutants. *La Revue canadienne des langues vivantes* 42, 3.

— (1990) *Étude nationale sur les programmes de français de base – Rapport synthèse.* Winnipeg: ACPLS et M Éditeur.

— (1992) Les programmes d'immersion et l'habileté à communiquer. *Études de linguistique appliquée* 88.

Long, M. (1983) Native speaker/non-native speaker conversation and the negotiation of comprehensible input. *Applied Linguistics* 4.

— (1985) Input and second language acquisition theory. In S. Gass and C. Madden (eds) *Input in Second Language Acquisition*. Rowley, MA: Newbury House.

Morley, J. (1984) *Listening and Language Learning in ESL*. Englewood Cliffs, NJ: Prentice-Hall.

Nord, J. (1978) Listening fluency before speaking: An alternative paradigm. Paper presented at the 1978 World Congress of AILA, Montreal.

O'Malley, J.M., Chamot, A.U. and Kupper, L. (1989) Listening comprehension strategies in second language acquisition. *Applied Linguistics* 10, 4.

Oxford, R.L. (1985) *A New Taxonomy of Second Language Learning Strategies*. Washington, DC: ERIC Clearinghouse.

— (1990) *Language Learning Strategies*. Boston, MA: Heinle & Heinle Publishers.

Painchaud, G. (1990) *Étude nationale sur les programmes de français de base: Le syllabus Langue*. Winnipeg: CASLT & M Éditeur.

Postovsky, V. (1972) The effects of teaching the receptive skills at the beginning of second language learning. Paper presented at the 1972 World Congress of AILA, Copenhagen.

— (1974) Effects of delay in oral practice at the beginning of second language learning. *Modern Language Journal* 56.

Richards, J. (1983) Listening comprehension: Approach, design, procedure. *TESOL Quarterly* 17, 2.

Smith, F. (1982) *Understanding Reading*. Hillsdale, NJ: Erlbaum.

Stern, H.H. (1984) L'immersion: Une expérience singulière. *Langue et Société* 12.

Tremblay, R., Duplantie, M. and Huot, D. (1990) *National Core French study – The Communicative-experiential Syllabus*. Winnipeg: ACPLS and M Éditeur.

Winitz, H. and Reeds, J.A. (1973) Rapid acquisition of foreign language (German) by the avoidance of speaking. *IRAL* 11, 4.

4 Developing Comprehension and Interaction Skills with Idiomatic Expressions

GEORGES DUQUETTE

This chapter proposes that idioms, culturally rooted and chunked as they are into units of speech, are useful in developing communicative competence. It proposes that communicative competence requires background context and cultural information so that skills are properly used. It also shows that idiomatic expressions are more likely to help students integrate functional speech because it taps more into that information than randomly selected words. The author presents a number of idioms which are grouped according to 10 different contexts in which the expressions may be used.

Introduction

Developing oral proficiency and literacy skills requires more than simply being able to speak and write. According to Edwards (1991), literacy means to understand the context and culture of the target language and to respond appropriately to its expectations.

This involves a lot of comprehensible input because comprehension precedes production and performance output is not greater than the input comprehension skills developed (Krashen and Terrell, 1983). A language needs to be first understood in the target context and culture in which it will be used. Without these context cues and cultural norms, sensory input for acquisition purposes may be insufficient.

Just as sensory input is necessary to cognition (Solso, 1988), contact with the real world is essential to the acquisition of socio-cultural skills (Fishman, 1989). Schools should focus more upon skills which are experienced in context and acquired in the real world, making sure also that any skill acquired in school is also transferable and transferred to the real world (Steinacker & Bell, 1979). Some studies have shown that communicative strategies which take into account background information (advanced organisers) are helpful to the acquisition of skills (Herron, 1994).

The purpose of this chapter is to help students recognise real situations where they will be called upon to use idiomatic expressions and to use these expressions appropriately. This will involve taking into account background information which may be relevant in defining a strategy.

Since experiences may vary from one student to another, the emphasis will be on student strategies, not specific tactics (Seliger, 1991). As a teacher, you may later wish to get students to add to their experiences by trying out their strategies in different situations. The following are only model expressions intended to 'jumpstart' your activities.

Theoretical Framework

How useful is the acquisition of idioms in helping students develop communicative competence? Some studies reported that idioms are helpful in developing communicative competence because:

(a)   a positive relationship exists between idioms processed into long-term memory and success on communicative tasks (Schuster-Webb, 1980);

(b)   idioms have regularity, are functional, and they present a stratificational view of language (Strässler, 1982);

(c)   idioms are more likely to be used with peers (Dickson, 1981).

The acquisition of idioms and other commonly used expressions give self-confidence to the L2 student by letting them successfully use these expressions with the target language group. Because cultural meaning may vary from one group to another (Hall, 1973) and that meaning is already built-into these expressions (Schuster-Webb, 1980), the L2 student gets the impression of using a phase that has already been 'well-coined' (so to speak) so as to enable him or her to be well understood.

Like a child acquiring a first language and who, at first, produces expressions whose mean length of utterance may be of one or two words, a L2 learner may use idioms by themselves to convey their affective, semantic, and linguistic meanings in a way that is easy for them to master and comprehensible to the target language group.

Afterwards, students may build upon or around idiomatic expressions. For example, results of an experiment (Ervin-Tripp, 1974) showed that an expression such as 'Get out of here' may, three months later, be integrated into a series of expressions such as 'Let's go! Get out of here! Let's get out of here'.

This paper rests on three principles of language acquisition which, in turn, are supported by a number of studies.

(a) Fishman (1989) has shown that language comprehension and language performance, to be meaningful, require context-defined cues and a socio-cultural framework in which communication can take place.

(b) Krashen (1993) demonstrates the importance of providing 'comprehensible input' to increase comprehension and facilitate the acquisition process.

(c) Giles and Coupland (1991) refer to integrative motivation or the identification process with the outgroup (target language group) and the ingroup (the student's home language group). Certain studies on group identity suggest that target group integration, acceptance and identification are important factors in developing communicative competence (Duquette & Cléroux, 1993; Erikson, 1980; Trueba, 1991).

Ongoing exposure and practice in using idioms with members of the target language group should help students increase their communicative competence in the target language. Since a second language learner has limited experience with the proposed new culture and language, he or she is at a disadvantage in at least three respects:

(a) The target culture and language may be quite different from one's previously acquired behaviour and language.

(b) Cultural experiences may be different in terms of perception, encoding, storage, retrieval and production (Solso, 1989).

(c) Cognitive development usually parallels the development of the first or most dominant language (Vygotsky, 1962).

In a sense, idioms seem to bridge this barrier because they are simple to grasp, frequently used, semantically and culturally-loaded, and target-culture rooted. In fact, 'one way to discover the attitudes of a people is to examine their idioms' (Chaika, 1982: 200).

Because a second language learner will tend to follow an ecclectic path between the cognitive, cultural, or linguistic expectations of both groups (Fantini, 1985) and to transfer language skills (Cummins, 1979) or develop interlanguage skills (Selinker, 1991), he or she is more likely to synchronise with the target group culture by using already well-defined expressions.

Classroom Strategies

At the outset, directions and explanations may be given in the students' first language in order to ensure that they understand well how the activities will develop. It is important always to remember that comprehensible input precedes production (Krashen, 1993) and that student comprehension must always be ensured.

However, once the students have acquired experience with these activities, the basic directions should, individually, when the need occurs and once comprehension has been ensured, be reiterated in the target language.

In order to help students acquire frequently used idioms, it is necessary first to identify the current habits of students, so an initial discussion on their habits is encouraged. Then, the target culture contexts in which these idioms many be used need to be presented. The best way is for teachers to present a short film (preferably in the target language) on the target culture group's habits. This sets the stage for possible behaviour adaptation or modification which may be needed by the students in using the target language.

The Activities

Teachers may divide the class into groups of two to four students and have them prepare and act out simulations. Smaller groups are recommended at first in order to keep the activity as simple as possible. Groups may gradually be enlarged as students successfully interact and act out these simulations.

Students should work with friends or someone with whom they feel comfortable. Together, they are asked to prepare a simulation in which they ask for something and are given a reply. The simulations should initially be kept very simple to maintain a comfortable classroom atmosphere and encourage student success. The length of the activity should be decided by the group so that the rhythm is natural and their progress gradual to the group. During this phase, the teacher acts as a resource person, helping students along as required.

Below is a list of English idioms under selected situations. However, as idioms are for the most part culturally defined and limited to the language in which they are used, these specific examples will no doubt be helpful only to teachers of English as a second language. Other second language teachers should select their own idioms in terms of their appropriateness in meeting student needs and potential for frequency of use, inviting students to use them as tools of communication, alternating between simulated classroom situations and real-life experiences.

Before introducing situations in which these idioms are used, teachers are urged to do the following:

- Since we learn through our senses and comprehensible input begins with sensory knowledge, expose your students to real-life experiences. Present some form of sensory input to the class in the form of a video, a guest speaker, a class visit to a supermarket or even a reading selection (with pictures) to provide students with concrete background world knowledge. This information will ensure that the discussion about communication is not done only in a vacuum (or abstract).
- Clarify with each group the objective of the exercise. For instance, are students to obtain directions, purchase stamps at the post office, ask a waitress for a cup of coffee, etc.?
- Elicit student strategies so they can decide how they will communicate in order to reach their objectives.

List of Idioms

(1) **mealtime**
   eat out, give a raincheck, go dutch, go to waste, have done with, head out, highway robbery, hit the spot, on the town, paint the town red, pick up the tab, throw a party, wet one's whistle.

(2) **purchases and sales**
   buy out, cash in, double check, figure out, flat broke, for a song, get by, in return, in the bag, in the black, in the red, on the sly, pay off, pick out, run up a bill, sacred cow, save for a rainy day, save up, scrape and save, set aside, under the counter.

(3) **relationships**
   beat around the bush, blow one's own horn, butt in, bring up, flip flop, forgive and forget, for the best, get across, get along, get a word in edgewise, give the benefit of the doubt, in private, last word, give a hard time, give ground, give in, lend an ear to, listen in, misty eyed, on one's behalf, once over, out in left field, out in the cold, out of touch, part company, pass over, pass the buck, patch up, pat on the back, perk up, play down, slip of the tongue, shoot the breeze, spitting image, take leave, take the cake, take the words out of one's mouth, take to heart, talk turkey, twist one's arm.

(4) **dating**
butt in or cut in, call up, carry a torch for, fall for, fond of, fooling
around, get the brushoff, give and take, good side of, go steady, go to
one's head, have an eye on, hit it off, let go, look for, looking forward
to, make up, miss out, on cloud nine, on the fence, on the rocks, one's
eye on, out of line, over with, play the field, put on hold, promise the
moon, sell short, skin deep, sleep on, slow down, spring chicken, spruce
up, sweep off one's feet, turn down, walk out.

(5) **opposition or conflict**
blow off steam, bone to pick, breathe down one's neck, bury the
hatchet, clear the air, face to face, face up to, flare up, forgive and forget,
frightened to death, get the jump on, get the last laugh, give a wide
berth, hang up, have had it, have the last word, in hot water, in one's
way, iron out, mean business, part company, pipe down, rock the boat,
sick and tired, smooth over, square off, stand up to, steer clear, stick to
one's guns, stir up a hornet's nest, strike out, stuck up, swinging one's
weight, take to task, take sides, talk back, through hell or high water,
throw one's weight around, throw up one's hands, up in arms, walk
out.

(6) **facing and resolving difficulties**
break through, bring to light, check it out, come to grips with, cry over
spilled milk, find out, get to the bottom of, get to the heart of, go to the
dogs, go to pieces, go through hell or high water, go off the deep end,
goose bumps or goose pimples, make head or tail, nothing to sneeze
at, on second thought, play it safe, rule out, seat of one's pants, skin of
one's teeth, soul searching, stick it out, take a turn for the worst, take
the wind out of one's sails, takes the cake, out on a limb, walk the floor.

(7) **bedtime**
bundle up, dead tired, forty winks, out like a light, shut eye, turn in.

(8) **getting around**
call upon, come over, dash off, drop in, get a move on, get around, get
hold of, get off, get to, go on, go over, in time, on time, know one's way
around, make it snappy, on the go, pick up, take leave, take time, travel
light.

(9) **employment**
at one's fingertips, bread and butter, brush up, by trial and error, call
down, call it a day, call it quits, catch up, come to grips with, fill out,
get ahead, get behind, get off the ground, get the jump on, have one's
hands full, hit the road, know one's way around, lead the way, nose to

the grindstone, on hand, on record, on the job, on track, out of order, over one's head, pitch in, pound the pavement, start from scratch, steal the show, stick it out, sweat of one's brow, take charge, take stock, to the bone, walking papers, wear one's self out, with heart and soul, working against the clock.

(10) **the outdoors, sports and hobbies**
bring up the rear, by a hair, by a long shot, by a mile, by inches, by leaps and bounds, camp out, cut across, goof off, in shape, in season, jump in, keep time, keep up, out of breath, out of shape, rough it, second breath, shape up, sign up, take turns, take it easy, warm up, work off, work out.

(11) **others**
come to light, down the drain, for crying out loud, get the picture, ghost of a chance, in the clear, in the dark, lose sight of, neither hide nor hair, no laughing matter, not at liberty to tell, on the cuff, on the other hand, on the spur of the moment, on the whole, on top of the world, once in a blue moon, play it by ear, safe and sound, scratch the surface, snap out of, so and so, song and dance, straight from the horse's mouth, time and again.

Follow up activities

While the following strategies may be practised in a classroom environment, the ultimate purpose is to have students try them out in 'real life' context situations. A teacher is encouraged to have students do 'real life' activities such as 'take the bus', 'make a shopping list and go shopping', 'call for directions', etc.

For writing purposes, teachers may also develop cloze tests or exercises. This involves a list of sentences and each sentence contains a blank space. The teacher lists the idioms at the bottom and the student chooses the idiom that belongs in each sentence.

References

Boatner, M.T. (1966) *A Dictionary of Idioms for the Deaf* (1st edn). Washington: Connecticut Printers.

Chaika, E. (1982) *Language: The Social Mirror*. Rowley, MA: Newbury House.

Cummins, J. (1979) Linguistic interdependence and the educational development of bilingual children. *Review of Educational Research* 49, 222–51.

Dickson, W.P. (1981) *Children's Oral Communication Skills*. New York: Academic Press.

Duquette, G and Cléroux, C. (1993) Vivre en milieu minoritaire. In G. Duquette (ed.) *Méthodes et strategies pour l'enseignement au secondaire.* Welland: Éditions Soleil.

Edwards, J. (1991) Literacy and education in contexts of cultural and linguistic heterogeneity. *The Canadian Modern Language Review/La Revue canadienne des langues vivantes* 47 (5), 933–49.

Erikson, E. (1980) *Identity and the Life Cycle.* New York: Norton.

Ervin-Tripp, (1974) Is second language learning like the first? *TESOL Quarterly* 8 (2), 111–28.

Fantini, A. (1985) *Language Acquisition of a Bilingual Child: A Sociolinguistic Perspective.* Clevedon: Multilingual Matters.

Fishman, J. (1989) *Language and Ethnicity in Minority Sociolinguistic Perspectives.* Clevedon: Multilingual Matters.

Giles, H. and Coupland, N. (1991) *Language, Contexts, and Consequences.* Milton Keynes: Open University Press.

Hall, E.T. (1973) *The Silent Language.* New York: Anchor Books.

Herron, C. (1994) An investigation of the effectiveness of using an advance organiser to introduce video in the foreign English classroom. *The Modern Language Journal* 78 (2), 190–8.

Krashen, S.D. (1993) The case for free voluntary reading. *The Canadian Modern Language Review* 50 (1), 72–82.

Krashen, S.D. and Terrell, T. (1983) *The Natural Approach: Language Acquisition in the Classroom.* Oxford: Pergamon.

Seliger, H. (1991) Strategy and tactics in second language acquisition. In L. Malavé and G. Duquette (eds) *Language, Culture and Cognition: A Collection of Studies in First and Second Language Acquisition.* Clevedon: Multilingual Matters.

Selinker, L. (1991) Along the way: Interlanguage systems in second language acquisition. In L. Malavé and G. Duquette (eds) *Language, Culture, and Cognition: A Collection of Studies in First and Second Language Acquisition.* Clevedon: Multilingual Matters.

Schuster-Webb, K. (1980) *A Study of Cognitive Processing Strategies for the Encoding of English Idioms into Long-term Memory.* Ann Arbor, MI: University Microfilms International.

Solso, R.I. (1988) *Cognitive Psychology.* Toronto: Allyn & Bacon.

Steinacker, N.W. and Bell, M.R. (1979) *The Experimental Taxonomy.* New York: Academic Press.

Strässler, J. (1982) *Idioms in English.* Germany: Gunter Narr Verlag Tubingen.

Trueba, H. (1991) Learning needs of minority children: Contributions of ethnography to educational research. In L. Malavé and G. Duquette (eds) *Language, Culture, and Cognition: A Collection of Studies in First and Second Language Acquisition.* Clevedon: Multilingual Matters.

Vygotsky, L.S. (1962) *Thought and Language.* Cambridge, MA: MIT Press.

5 Strategies for Developing Communicative Competence with Emphasis on Comprehensible Input

JOAN NETTEN and JANETTE PLANCHAT-FERGUSON

This chapter addresses the problem of using a communicative approach with beginning second language learners. Four major requirements for successful instruction are discussed: the need to teach language form in a functional context; the need to provide L2 input that is comprehensible to the student; the need to develop interaction in the classroom which is as authentic as possible; and the need to engage students in production of the target language. The importance of teaching strategies which permit the negotiation of both meaning and form, and the use of reference questions to make communication more realistic is emphasised. The use of learning tasks which involve the student intellectually as well as linguistically is recommended and examples are given.

The objective of this chapter is primarily to assist teachers of students at the early levels of second language instruction to conceptualise more clearly their role as facilitators of communication. In particular, this chapter has as its specific objectives to demonstrate the need of providing beginning students with:

- comprehensible input in the form of short sentences, phrases, and relatively simple language segments which are integrated into activities of purposeful communication;
- situations/exchanges which are as authentic as possible, bringing about a maximum of personal involvement in the communication despite limited language resources; and

- opportunities to use the target language in social interactions which allow the student choice in using a variety of simple linguistic forms to convey a message in a particular situational context.

Second language acquisition theory gives support to the view that the target language is best learned for communicative purposes by using it. Research studies have indicated that learning a second or a foreign language occurs in a remarkably similar fashion to that of first language learning (Hawkins & Towell, 1992). The brain appears to be, to a certain extent, 'programmed' to learn language. Linguistic features peculiar to the way a language works are extrapolated while the learner is attending to the message being conveyed. It must surely be obvious to any teacher that a language is far too complex for all its aspects to be taught item by item. In teaching a second or a foreign language, hereafter referred to as L2, we must rely, at least in part, on the capacity of the mind to learn a certain amount of what is called the grammar of the language while the learner is intellectually involved in deciphering a message.

There is, however, a need to add to this process by assisting the learner to observe characteristic features of the L2 more effectively, and to recognise and correct errors. Such instruction makes the language learning process more efficient, particularly for older learners (Doughty, 1991).

Based on these considerations, a distinction has been made between language acquisition and language learning: acquisition tending to refer to the learning of the language through use, which focuses on meaning; and learning referring to the effects of instruction which focuses on the linguistic code or form of L2 (Krashen & Terrell, 1983). Neither process on its own, however, appears to be sufficient if the end result is to be the development of both fluency and accuracy in the use of the L2. Indeed, in natural language learning situations both learning and acquisition regularly occur simultaneously (Germain, 1991: 50). To attempt to distinguish between the two, particularly at the early stages of L2 instruction, may create an artificial separation that impedes understanding the L2 acquisition process.

L2 Learning Tasks

Even at the very early stages of the development of target language competence, it is necessary for students to participate in short conversational exchanges that are somewhat free in nature. At this stage, students should be able to:

- understand a brief message of no more than one or two short sentences in length;
- reply to a question or a comment with a short sentence, phrase, or appropriate word;
- request information by using a short question, comment, phrase, or appropriate word;
- use appropriate socio-linguistic forms; and
- use appropriate idiomatic expressions, particularly those which are a part of ordinary/regular oral exchanges.

The achievement of these goals demands the utilisation of short messages and question/answer sequences which require a limited target language repertoire, yet which can be used in a variety of communicative activities. However, the learning tasks must leave the student with the initiative to choose appropriate L2 items to reach a communication goal. Choice of the language items to be used by the speaker is an essential characteristic of real communication.

Principle 1: Situational Context

The situational context in which the L2 instruction occurs is important for three reasons. It provides the communicative goals without which L2 learning is less likely to take place. Secondly, it provides the motivational incentive within which the language acquisition process operates more effectively. Thirdly, it provides a framework which aids the student's comprehension of the message. Thus it provides the means by which the student deciphers, consciously and unconsciously, how the language works.

The teaching of grammar rules for L2, particularly when expressed in the somewhat abstruse language of the linguist, has been shown to be of limited usefulness to the student (Hagen & Dewitt, 1993). In the communicative approach, the amount of formal grammar instruction is considerably reduced. Language instruction focusing on form does not need to precede communicative language use, but appears to be most effective if it occurs within a functional/situational context (Day & Shapson, 1991) and is integrated into interactive exchanges with the student which focus on meaning (Lyster, 1994). In this view, formal language instruction encompasses any activity/interchange which has as its goal to heighten the student's awareness of the phonological, morphological syntactic, and lexical features of L2.

Situation 1: Introduction/Name

Content organisation: Situational context – learning names.

Major strategies: Integration of formal language instruction in functional context.

- Variety of simple comprehensible input.

Example: Language forms: Je m'appelle... (My name is...)
                                    Tu t'appelles... (your name is...)
                                    Il s'appelle... (his name is...)
                                    Elle s'appelle... (her name is...)

Presentation

(1) Teacher introduces self: Je m'appelle Janette (My name is Janette).
(2) Teacher elicits other examples:
     (a) Et toi? Quel est ton nom? (And you, what is your name?)
     (b) Comment t'appelles-tu? (What do you call yourself?)
     (c) Tu t'appelles? (You are called?)
     (d) Veux-tu te présenter à la classe? (Would you present yourself to the class?)
(3) Teacher extends examples by asking some students to identify other students in the class.
     (a) Et lui? Sais-tu comment il s'appelle? (And him, do you know what he calls himself?)
     (b) Tu la connais? Comment s'appelle-t-elle? (And her, do you know what she calls herself?)

Principle 2: Comprehensible Input

The student should be provided with as much comprehensible input as possible. Language is so intricate that it would be impossible to teach formally, or analytically, all the knowledge necessary to use it fluently and accurately. Therefore, it is necessary to expose the students to as much target language as possible, thus permitting them to process language data unconsciously, and consequently learn, so to speak, much more than can be taught. Furthermore, the learner must be provided with authentic language from which good data about L2 morphology and syntax can be acquired.

While the link between comprehension and acquisition has not yet been proven by research (Lightbown & Spada, 1993: 28), the degree to which the student can comprehend the message appears to affect the amount of linguistic data which can be interpreted from the message at the same time. This relationship creates a need for somewhat simplified messages, if the process is to work effectively at the beginning stage of L2 instruction, since each message contains large amounts of linguistic data for the student to process while absorbing the message. The use of this strategy, sometimes called 'caretaker language', is reported in the early stages of all language learning. Research in French immersion classrooms has shown that L2 achievement is higher in classrooms where teachers acknowledged some simplification of the L2 forms used (Netten, 1991). However, it has also been established that simplification of the message is less important than establishing comprehension through interaction with the learner. This process, referred to as negotiating meaning, appears to be particularly beneficial to the development of competence in L2 (Ellis, 1986).

Situation 2: Directions

Content organisation: Language function: Giving directions.
Major strategies: Comprehensible input and negotiation of meaning.
Example: Lexical item – tout droit.

(A) *Preparation for activity*

(1) Prepare a simplified map. Have an enlarged copy which may be used for whole class activities, or a transparency. Have individual copies available for small group activities.
(2) Have several items located on the maps; e.g. bank, drugstore, post office, park, school, church, cinema.
(3) A list of phrases with arrows indicating the meaning can also be distributed.
(4) Teacher uses these materials to locate items on the map, and have students locate items.

(B) *Presentation*

T: Pour te rendre/aller à l'école, en quelle direction faut-il aller? À droite ou à gauche?
S: Tout droit.
T: Tout droit? Si je marche tout droit, je me trouve à l'église.
S₁: Droit?
S₂: A droite?
T: Il faut marcher à droite. Et pour aller de l'école au bureau de poste?
S₁: A droite.
T: Cependant, pour aller de l'école à la banque?
S₁&₂: Tout droit.

The negotiation process can also be extended to L2 form as well as meaning (See examples in Lyster, 1994). This strategy aids both comprehension and the development of accuracy in L2.

Principle 3: Authentic Communication

Communication theorists have indicated that real communication requires both choice of language on the part of the speaker and an information gap. There must be some knowledge in the exchange that is not already known to one of the participants. This means that there must be real communicative intent for the interchange to be valuable as a L2 learning tool. Studies have shown how unauthentic L2 classroom language tends to be (White & Lightbown, 1984). The use of questions by the teacher to which the answer is not already known are helpful in creating authentic communication in the classroom (Long & Sato, 1983). Germain *et al.* (1991) provide many useful suggestions for making classroom communication more authentic.

Situation 3: Personal likes/dislikes

Content organization: Thematic.

Major strategies: Use of referential questions, i.e. answer not known.
                       Conversational interaction.

Example: Qu'est-ce que tu aimes/détestes?

Presentation

T: Moi, j'aime le chocolat, mais je déteste les chien-chauds/hot dogs.
       Et toi, Lucille? Qu'est-ce que tu aimes?

S: Le coke.

T: Moi aussi, mais je préfère le pepsi.
       Henri, qu'aimes-tu?/qu'est-ce que tu aimes?

S: J'aime les hamburgers.

T: Et toi, Jean? Tu les aimes, aussi?

S: Non, Je les déteste.

In order for the language acquisition process, as it may be called, to operate effectively, the student must be intellectually involved in the communicative interchange. Marginal involvement appears to reduce linguistic data processing. Intellectual involvement and participation with communicative intent can probably best be achieved through the use of content-oriented instruction. Thus, the solving of a mathematical problem, participation in a simple scientific experiment, or determining a means of caring for the environment are types of activities which enhance the development of L2. At the early stages of instruction, where these types of activities are more difficult to implement because of the paucity of the L2 language repertoire, learning tasks with specific communicative goals, such as the resolution of a problem rather than a general discussion (Duff, 1986) and those which provide each student with a specific task, particularly that of providing information not available to others (Pica & Doughty, 1988) tend to contribute most effectively to the development of L2.

Situation 4: Introduction of students in class

Content organisation: Situational context – introductions; exchange of personal information.
Major strategies: Language choice within limited resources.
Specific task assignment for each student.
Intellectual and personal involvement of students.

(A) *Preparation for activity*

    (1) Teacher has used/taught the questions such as:
        (a) Comment t'appelles-tu?/Quel est ton nom?/Et toi?
        (b) Que comptes-tu faire comme carrière/profession/métier?
        (c) Qu'est-ce que tu aimes/détestes?

(B) *Presentation of activity*

    (1) Teacher introduces self: Je m'appelle Janette.
                                  Je suis professeur.
                                  J'aime le chocolat.
    (2) Teacher elicits other examples by asking some students to introduce selves. 'Veux-tu te présenter à la classe?' 'Et toi?'

(C) *Activity*

    (1) Students choose a partner.
    (2) Student A elicits profile of student B; Student B elicits profile of Student A. (Notes may be taken. Guidelines may be placed on board.)
    (3) Students return to whole class situation. (Can sit in circle.)
    (4) Student A introduces Student B and makes an incorrect statement. Class must determine which statement is incorrect.

(D) *Teaching strategies*

   (1) Students are placed in a situation which is of some personal interest, and in which each must use the L2 for a specific task.

   (2) Some degree of intellectual involvement is required to listen to and remember information about their partner or other classmates.

   (3) Choice of questions and responses becomes available to the students within a very limited language repertoire.

Principle 4: L2 Practice

Practice in L2 production is most effective if organised into small group or other types of cooperative learning activities (Long & Porter, 1985; Wells, 1981, 1985). Cognitive psychology suggests that social interaction acts as a stimulant to learning. In addition, the use of these organisational forms enhances the number of opportunities each student has to communicate (Netten & Spain, 1989) and increases the possibilities for the negotiation of meaning (Duff, 1986), therefore contributing substantially to L2 development. The use of role-play and other forms of improvisational educational drama can also be useful. Well-structured role-plays and dramatisations enable students to participate in an imagined situation and use language creatively.

At the beginning level, simple activities with a communicative intent must be sufficiently structured to enable the student to convey a message with an economy of words, since the vocabulary and other linguistic resources of the student are limited at this point. Accordingly, learning tasks need to be carefully planned in order to ensure that the students possess all the linguistic data necessary to enable them to proceed independently and effectively. However, the L2 learning tasks in which the students participate should be so constructed as to leave the students choice in the manner in which they respond to and reach the communicative goal. In this way the students practise drawing on their language competencies in order to communicate a message and, as a result are involved in learning experiences which have some of the characteristics of authentic communication. The teacher should ensure that students learn more than one appropriate form for the language functions being explored, giving attention to socio-linguistic considerations whenever warranted. The reliance on short, simple language forms also contributes to L2 accuracy, and the comprehensibility of the output.

This early stage of L2 learning is the time to encourage students to draw on all their resources, to take risks in the language, and to use communicative strategies in order to bring the interchange to a satisfactory communicative end. As the student matures in language competence, communication strategies which reduce accuracy can gradually be refined (Lyster, 1994).

Situation 5: Où se trouve la banque?

Content organisation: Situational context/Language function – asking for and giving directions.

Major strategies: Intellectual involvement of students in problem solving.

Information gap – one student possesses information needed by another student.

Negotiation of meaning between students.

(A) *Activity*

(1) Students are divided into pairs or small groups. Only half of the students have maps.

(2) Student A asks directions to a particular place. Student B, who possesses a map, provides a reply.

(3) Student A goes to another Student B and asks directions.

(4) The activity is repeated until each Student A has had several occasions to request directions.

(5) Maps and roles are reversed, and the activity continues.

(B) *Possible exchanges*

La banque Royale, s.v.p. (The Royal Bank, please.)	Tout droit, madame/à droite/à gauche. (Straight ahead, madam/to the right/to the left.)
Où est la pharmacie? (Where is the drug store?)	Là-bas, monsieur. Juste en face. (Over there, sir. Straight ahead.)
Je cherche l'église. (I'm looking for the church.)	Je ne sais pas. (I don't know.)
Où se trouve l'école secondaire? (Where is the high school?)	Je m'excuse, mais je ne sais pas. (I'm sorry, but I don't know.)

Est-ce qu'il y a un bureau de poste près d'ici? (Is there a post office near here?)	Je ne peux pas te le dire. (I'm unable to tell you.)
	Je ne suis pas d'ici. (I am not from here.)

(C) *Extension of activity*

(1) Students select a partner. One student possesses a list of places; the other student possesses a copy of the map where the places are located.

(2) Student A asks directions to various places. Student B replies.

(3) Students reverse roles and the activity continues.

(4) Students switch partners and continue the activity.

Note: A map of the local area, or a city the students might visit (e.g. Montreal) is used.

Language production is also useful in developing the learners' awareness of the language repertoire available to them, thus personalising the L2 learning process. Through involvement in interactive activities, the student realises what s/he does not know and needs to know in order to cope in a particular situation, contributing to motivating subsequent learning. In addition, the use of the L2 in communicative situations demonstrates to the students the adequacy of their knowledge of the linguistic code, enabling them to benefit considerably more from formal language instruction. Learning can thus become more self-directed and focused, and is, as a consequence, more effective.

The learning of a language centres around the use of the language for communicative purposes, and the gradual refinement of the communicative tool to express in a more and more educated fashion concepts of increasing intellectual sophistication. At the beginning, only the germ of this ultimate goal is present, but the communicative intent of language learning must be nurtured as it assists the student to understand both the purpose and the means of L2 acquisition.

References

Day, E. and Shapson, S. (1991) Integrating formal and functional approaches in language teaching in French immersion: An experimental study. *Language Learning* 41 (1), 25–58.

Doughty, C. (1991) Second language instruction does make a difference. *Studies in Second Language Acquisition* 13, 431–69.

Duff, P.A. (1986) Another look at interlanguage talk: Talking task to task. In R.R. Day (ed.) *Talking to Learn: Conversation in Second Language Acquisition*. Rowley, MA: Newbury House.

— (1988) *Teaching English*. Cambridge: Cambridge University Press.

Ellis, R. (1986) *Understanding Second Language Acquisition*. Oxford: Oxford University Press.

Germain, C. (1991) *Le point sur l'approche communicative en didactique des langues*. Anjou (Québec): Centre éducatif et culturel, inc.

Germain, C., Hardy, M. and Pambianchi, G. (1991) *Interaction enseignant(e)/élèves*. Anjou (Québec): Centre éducatif et culturel, inc.

Hagen, L.K. and Dewitt, J. (1993) Teaching French cleft constructions to English speakers: What syntactic theory has to say. *Canadian Modern Language Review* 49 (3), 550–66.

Hawkins, R. and Towell, R. (1992) Second language acquisition research and the second language acquisition of French. *French Language Studies* 2, 97–121.

Krashen, S.D. and Terrell, T.D. (1983) *The Natural Approach: Language Acquisition in the Classroom*. New York: Pergamon Press.

Lightbown, P.M. and Spada, N. (1993) *How Languages are Learned*. Oxford: Oxford University Press.

Long, M.H. and Porter, P.A. (1985) Group work, interlanguage talk and second language acquisition. *TESOL Quarterly* 19, 207–28.

Long, M.H. and Sato, C.J. (1983) Classroom foreign talk discourse: Forms and functions of teacher questions. In H.W. Seliger and M.H. Long (eds) *Classroom Oriented Research in Second Language Acquisition*. Rowley, MA: Newbury House.

Lyster, R. (1994) La négotiation de la forme: Stratégie analytique en classe d'immersion. *La Revue Canadiane des langues vivantes* 50 (3), 1–20.

— (1990) The role of analytic language teaching in French immersion programs. *The Canadian Modern Language Review* 47 (1), 101–17.

Netten, J. (1991) Towards a more language oriented second language classroom. In L.M. Malavé and G. Duquette (eds) *Language, Culture and Cognition* (pp. 284–304). Clevedon: Multilingual Matters.

Netten, J. and Spain, W.H. (1989) Student/teacher interaction patterns in the French immersion classroom: Implications for levels of achievement in French language proficiency. *The Canadian Modern Language Review* 45 (3), 485–501.

Pica, T. and Doughty, C. (1988) Variations in classroom interaction as a function of participation pattern and task. In J. Fine (ed.) *Second Language Discourse: A Textbook of Current Research*. Norwood, NJ: Ablex Publishing. Cited in Germain (1991).

Wells, G. (1981) Language as interaction: The study of language development. In G. Wells (ed.) *Learning through Interaction* (pp. 22–72). Cambridge: Cambridge University Press.

— (1985) Language and learning: An interactional perspective. In G. Wells and J. Nicholls (eds) *Language and Learning: An Interactional Perspective* (pp. 21–39). London: The Falmer Press.

White, J. and Lightbown, P.M. (1984) Asking and answering in ESL classes. *The Canadian Modern Language Review* 40 (2), 228–44.

6 Integrating Communication and Social Skills Using Ensemble Techniques

HANA SVAB and TED MILTENBERGER

During my early university years I decided to study Spanish and Russian. Because I already had a solid background in both Romance and Slavic languages, neither of these two languages seemed difficult to me, and three years later I could be considered quite proficient at communicating in both. When I entered the working world, my career took me to such places as Switzerland and Morocco, where I 'picked up' conversational Italian and broken Arabic respectively. Today, however, I can no longer converse in either of the two languages I learned at university, yet I can still function effectively in Italian and easily recall key phrases in Arabic.

Hana Svab

Krashen (1982) would undoubtedly say that learning Spanish and Russian in an artificial setting is quite different from acquiring Italian and Arabic in its own environment. Though Krashen's Monitor Theory has come under fire more than once, 'there is something important behind it' (Spolsky, 1989: 47).

Clyne (1985) studied two groups of German-speaking students learning English in a secondary school. Both groups were taught by the same teacher. In programme A, the teacher used the communicative approach to promote subconscious acquisition, and in programme B she used a more traditional approach to promote conscious learning. Though Clyne's findings may hardly come as a surprise to those who have successfully implemented communicative strategies in their own classrooms, it is nevertheless astonishing to see the extent to which the two groups differ in their performance.

In terms of numerical results, students in programme A performed better in every test (sound discrimination, listening comprehension, speaking, cloze, dictation and grammar), and significantly better overall in practically every skill (Clyne, 1985: 201).

A necessary ingredient in communicative teaching is the importance of helping students to make connections between what they are asked to do in class and what they already know. In his article, Nunan (1987) clearly demonstrates the results of his study on this topic. He provides us with actual transcripts that show different methods the language teacher used to elicit responses from her students. In the first case, the questions required a basic yes/no answer; in the second case, the questions were referential, requiring the students to draw upon previously acquired knowledge, past experience and cultural background. As could be expected, the students that put forth the greatest effort and, therefore, met with the greatest success, were those in the latter group, where communication held real meaning for them.

Second language acquisition implies the use of the target language as a *medium* and not as an *object* of instruction. In the interest of producing students who command excellent communication skills, we must also produce students who are competent in their social skills – one cannot comfortably exist without the other. Furthermore, if we consider the fact that the classroom is an apprenticeship for later authentic communication (Breen, 1985: 152), then we must ensure that all classroom communication be as genuine as possible. Students must be given the opportunity to react in the *target* language to situations that they would realistically encounter in various social settings; the sole use of the target language is a crucial factor, as research has proven over and over again that the process of translation acts as an intervening variable in intercultural [and interpersonal] interaction (Banks & Banks, 1991: 182).

The Ensemble Technique

The ensemble technique, adapted from the International Schools Theatre Association's approach to building Theatre Ensembles, emphasises developing a group 'synergy' which creates work results stronger than those of each member working at her or his best.

Because of their nature, ensemble techniques lend themselves perfectly to the integration of communication and social skills, simply because that is precisely what they are all about. Contrary to cooperative learning, there are no individual winners and no concrete rewards; however, the group's accomplishments, brought about through the students' combined efforts, will most certainly make the experience worthwhile. As in the educational theatre approach, ensemble work focuses on the student and on the learning process rather than on the end product. Students are taught to focus on themselves as they interact with and contribute to the group, to learn to function in a given society by assessing and modifying their own behaviour, and to take pride in the community they help to create. Also fostered is an acute awareness of the environment and of others around them. In a culturally diverse group of learners, ensemble techniques are particularly useful, as they capitalise on the strengths of a rich assortment of knowledge. Zich (1986: 2) explains the process:

> A strong Ensemble is created by establishing an atmosphere in which each individual is appreciated for her own merits. She is encouraged to share creatively with others. She is both supported by, and supports, others… [she] **is** an essential part of the production… there is commitment on the part of **all** performers… the teacher role becomes that of collaborator, not superior.

The remainder of this chapter will describe specific ensemble techniques (which have been especially well received in L2 courses at the intermediate level) and which teachers may like to try with their students. These techniques are not necessarily meant to be followed to the letter, nor must they always take place in the classroom. Any adaptations that individual teachers choose to make for the activity to work for a particular need should be tried.

The proposed activities generally increase in both length and complexity, with the initial ones building social skills and the latter ones using them. The order of activities can be shifted around to suit particular situations, though teachers with a beginning group of students may find it more useful to start with the simpler or shorter ones. No time limits are prescribed, as the outcome of each activity depends completely on the number of students participating, and on the particular characteristics of the group itself. The teacher should try to offer a wide array of activities that emphasise several different communication skills during each learning session.

Please note that the hints and activities which follow have been borrowed in part from Zich (1986).

A few hints before we begin

(1) Do encourage students to try, but never force them to do anything they do not want to do. Use students who sit out of exercises as those who can offer input to others by observing what is being done.

(2) Ensemble should be a positive learning experience – refrain from using negative words such as 'but' or 'no'. Come with the belief that everyone has something to offer to the group.

(3) Let mistakes happen. Students will not only learn from them but also demonstrate to others the importance of doing or not doing something.

(4) Consider having students keep Dialogue Journals. These are similar to diaries in that they are used by the students to record their feelings and reactions to their experiences in the classroom. The teacher then collects them at certain intervals, and offers the students informal, written comments on their content.

(5) Consider asking the students to write a personal letter to you at the end of the semester, in which they explain what they have learned from the ensemble and how they have grown as a result.

(6) Consider negotiating with your administration to have the course graded on a Pass/Fail basis with comments. This will help to alleviate tension that could be detrimental to the success of your endeavours.

(7) Do warmup and warmdown exercises to excite or relax students as needed.

(8) Provide a feeling of freedom and space, but always stay in control. Be prepared but flexible. If an activity needs to be stopped, stop it. If a student needs to calm down, allow him to step outside until he is ready to continue.

(9) If you have an odd number of students for an exercise, do not just ask someone to sit out and watch – ask him to be your helper or an observer, and find something meaningful for him to do. Try to offer this alternative to students who feel uncomfortable participating in certain exercises, too.

(10) Be especially aware of peer pressure, and of cultural and religious differences among students. Initially, it may be a wise tactic to have students of the same culture or religion work together.

(11) Do allow students to offer suggestions during the activities.

(12) Do explain to students *why* they are doing something, but be careful not to overkill.

(13) Feel free to use your own preferred follow-up methods (for example, supplementary reading, creative writing, class discussion, etc.) to provide definite closure at the end of each class.

(14) Do not underestimate the importance of silence and body language – they are often more powerful than the spoken word.

Activities

(1) Introduction interviews

Each student pairs up with another student he does not know. The students interview each other not only to ask about names, ages and addresses, but also to learn about interests, favourite foods, interesting experiences, etc. Each student then introduces his partner to the class, including as much information about him as he can remember.

(2) Customised alphabet

The students sit in a circle on the floor. One student starts by naming something that is important to him or his culture that begins with that letter (for example, Arabic, acting, affection, etc.). The second person must repeat what the first person said, and add on what is important to him or his culture that begins with the letter B.

The activity continues as above, with each student repeating what the others have already said. After four words, the activity must start again.

(3) Something in common

The students sit on chairs in a circle, with one student standing in the middle without a chair.

The student in the centre names something that some of the other students may have in common (for example, your name begins with a vowel, you are wearing red socks, you like bananas, etc.).

Those students that have that particular item in common must get up and change seats, while the student in the centre also looks for a seat. The student that is left without a seat is the next one in the centre.

(4) Ping-Pong

The students stand in pairs.

The teacher names a category that is rich in vocabulary (for example, objects associated with Christmas, polite refusals, directions, etc.), and the students in each group exchange words or phrases back and forth that fit the given category.

When the pair can no longer continue, the students remain silent until everyone else is also silent. The teacher suggests new categories as each one is exhausted.

(5) Body language

The teacher prepares a box full of slips of paper with simple instructions on them.

Each student draws a piece of paper from the box, and attemps to get the other students to do what is written on it. The student must not speak, nor may he explicitly exemplify the action himself. The students then sit down and explain what they had been asked to do.

Examples
The students must take off their shoes and line them up in the hallway.
The students must pretend they are riding horses on a racetrack.
The students must recite three nursery rhymes as a chorus.

(6) Family photos
Groups of six to eight students stand up in front of the rest of the class to pose for family photos.

The teacher chooses themes for the group to enact (for example, The Loving Family, The Skinny Family, The Canadian Family, etc.). A discussion regarding stereotyping is a good way to end this exercise.

(7) Group problem-solving
The students are asked to perform a series of actions that will require the assistance of at least one other person in the group. Each student must find a way to accomplish each task by eliciting help from the others.

All of this is to be done with imaginary objects, and it is important for the teacher or facilitator to see what is being mimed. The idea is to build the exercise to the point of requiring the group to work together in order to be successful.

Examples
Sew a button on an imaginary shirt, paying as much attention to detail as possible.
Wrap up a large package without using tape or glue.
Hang clothes on a clothesline that does not string up across the whole room.
Tie up a piano and attach it to a hook to transport it.
Move the rope to tie up an ocean liner from one corner of the room to the dock at the other corner of the room.

To develop communicative competence once an activity has been mimed, students develop conversations to accompany the activities.

(8) Add-ons
The students initially all sit as the audience.

One person stands up and begins to set a theme, either through mime or conversation (for example, he may pretend to be at the circus, in a supermarket, on an airplane, etc.).

As each of the other students comes to understand where the scene is taking place, he joins in by interacting in some way with the other student or students that are already on the scene. Each scene builds until all students are included in some way in the action.

(9) Theme machine

All students are initially sitting down as part of the audience.

The teacher names a theme (for example, tourists, sports, Africa, etc.) that the students must portray in the form of a machine. One person begins a movement and sound (may be a word or phrase) that seems typical to him of that particular theme. The next student finds some way to link on to the first student with a complementary movement and sound to further develop the given theme.

One by one, other students join in, to produce a machine of continuous movement and sound.

(10) Gibberish commercials

The students work in groups of three to five.

Each group prepares a commercial for a new product, which is to be presented to the class using gestures, gibberish and sounds only.

The rest of the students must then try to explain what the product is and what its benefits are. To develop communicative competence, this commercial is then re-enacted using words.

(11) Story board

Groups of five or six students get together to plan a story that could be told in seven or eight still film frames.

One person in the group asks the other students in the class, the audience, to close their eyes. While the audience's eyes are closed, the story group gets into a still position for the viewing of its first frame.

The other students are then told to open their eyes to take in the picture. When they are again told to close their eyes, the story group moves into another still position for the viewing of its second frame.

The steps continue as above until the students in the audience have viewed all the frames. The class is then asked to recount the story verbally.

(12) Chairs

The students are all sitting down, facing a chair that is at the front of the class.

The teacher calls out a character and a situation, and a student must then walk up to and sit down on that chair in the role of that character in that situation.

Examples

You are an elderly person. That is your favourite rocking chair.

You are a member of the royal family. That is your throne.

You are an unruly child in a museum. That is a priceless antique.

(13) Facial expressions

The students take turns expressing various emotions through their facial movements. The audience must try to describe how the performing student is feeling, and suggest a situation that may have caused him to feel this way.

(14) Public/private face

Half of the class stands up to perform while the other half of the class acts as the audience. The students standing up must turn their backs to the audience.

The teacher gives the students emotionally charged situations they must react to. The students turn around a first time to show how they would react in public, then turn around a second time to show how they would react in private.

Examples

You are at an important function and discover a terribly obvious stain on the front of your outfit.

You called in sick to work to go out with someone you have been wanting to date for a long time, and you unexpectedly meet your boss at the theatre.

You are at the hospital and happen to run into a person you do not like very much. She is in a wheelchair because she has broken her leg.

(15) Persuasion

The students pair up. The teacher gives the students directions as to what each student must try to convince the other student to do (for example, to give him a piece of gum, lend him some money, allow him to smoke in a non-smoking area, etc.), and the students take turns trying to coax each other into doing it. A variation is to give each student a conflicting goal without telling the other student.

(16) Complaints and praise

The students stand in front of the class, one by one.

Each student must take his turn at complaining about something, and then at talking very favourably about something. The complaints must all be completely negative, and the comments completely positive.

(17) Find your partners

The teacher prepares a box full of pairs of descriptions of situations, each written on a separate slip of paper.

Each student draws a slip of paper from the box and enacts the described situation. The students continue to follow these instructions as they try to find the person who seems to have the same instructions. Once the students have found each other, they sit down and wait for the others to finish.

Examples

You cannot hear well, but you do not want anyone to know.

You have just won a fortune in a lottery, but you are trying to keep it a secret.

You have lost a very valuable necklace, so you do not want anyone to notice that you are looking for it.

(18) Doors

Two or more students at a time are chosen or volunteer to perform for the rest of the class. One student must be behind the classroom door while the other student must open it each time the first person knocks.

Each time the student behind the door knocks and the door is opened for him, he must pretend to be a different character. In response, the second student takes on the role of another character that could respond to the first.

Examples

A door-to-door salesman and a housewife.

A policeman and a teenager guilty of speeding.

Your neighbour, who needs to borrow something.

The audience must then try to guess who the performing students were portraying, and what the nature of their relationship is.

(19) Language change

The students sit together in pairs or groups, and begin conversing using any style of language they wish (for example, formal or informal). The teacher then asks the students to switch the language style to suit varying situations, and the students respond accordingly.

Examples

Your grandmother just walked into the room.

You are on stage in front of the whole class.

You are with your girlfriend or boyfriend.

(20) **Limited space improvisation**

Four students at a time are asked to come into a small square (about 1.5 × 1.5 m) taped off on the floor. The teacher gives the students a situation on which they must then immediately build an improvised scene.

Examples

You are stuck in an elevator. One of you is a pregnant woman, one is a model on her way to an important interview, another is a small boy going to the dentist, and the last is the building's cleaning lady.

You are quadruplets in a crib with only one toy to play with.

You are astronauts in a space capsule that is lost.

(21) **Experts**

Two students are initially chosen or volunteer to sit on a panel of experts on a silly subject (for example, invisible office buildings). These experts sit on chairs beside each other, facing the rest of the class, their audience.

The audience asks the experts questions on the topic at hand, and the experts answer them. The experts must always disagree with each other, but must also remain polite.

(22) **Conversations about nothing**

The students sit on the floor, in pairs, facing one another.

The teacher gives the students a tantalising starter sentence, which one of the partners in each group repeats to the other. The second partner responds, and a conversation between the two follows. The students must avoid mentioning anything specific that they may actually be talking about.

Examples

She told me not to tell anyone.

I can't believe he said that to you.

It's all your fault.

References

Banks, A. and Banks, S.P. (1991) Translation in interpersonal communication. *International and Intercultural Communication Annual* XV, 171–85.

Breen, M.P. (1985) The social context for language learning: A neglected situation? *Studies in Second Language Acquisition* 7 (2), 135–58.

Celce-Murcia, M. and Larsen-Freeman, D. (1983) *The Grammar Book: An ESL/EFL Teacher's Course*. Boston, MA: Heinle and Heinle.

Cherryholmes, C.H. (1988) *Power and Criticism: Poststructural Investigations in Education*. New York: Teachers College Press

Clyne, M.G. (1985) Medium or object: Different contexts of (school-based) language acquisition. In K. Hytenstam and M. Pienemann (eds) *Modelling and Assessing Second Language Acquisition*. Clevedon: Multilingual Matters.

Cross, D. (1991) *A Practical Handbook of Language Teaching*. London: Cassell.

Ellis, R. and Whittington, D. (1981) *A Guide to Social Skill Training*. London: Croom Helm.

Gardner, P.C. (1985) *Social Psychology and Second Language Learning: The Role of Attitudes and Motivation*. London: Edward Arnold.

Harbord, J. (1992) The use of the mother tongue in the classroom. *English Language Teaching Journal* 46 (4), 352–5.

Heltai, P. (1989) Teaching vocabulary by oral translation. *English Language Teaching Journal* 43 (4), 288–93.

Horwitz, E.K. and Young, D.J. (1991) *Language Anxiety: From Theory and Research to Classroom Implications*. Englewood Cliffs, NJ: Prentice-Hall.

Johnston, P.H. (1992) *Constructive Evaluation of Literate Activity*. White Plains, NY: Longman.

Kim, J.H. (1991) Intercultural communication competence. *International and Intercultural Communication Annual* XV, 259–75.

— (1991) Influence of language and similarity on initial intercultural interaction. *International and Intercultural Communication Annual* XV, 213–29.

Krashen, S.D. (1982) *Principles and Practice in Second Language Acquisition*. Oxford: Pergamon Institute of English.

Laufer, B. and Eliasson, S. (1993) What causes avoidance in L2 learning. *Studies in Second Language Acquisition* 15 (1), 35–48.

McDonough, S.H. (1981) *Psychology in Foreign Language Teaching*. London: George Allen & Unwin.

Nunan, D. (1987) Communicative language teaching: Making it work. *English Language Teaching Journal* 41 (2), 136–45.

Oser, F.K., Dick, A. and Patry, J.-L. (eds) (1992) *Effective and Responsible Teaching: The New Synthesis*. San Francisco, CA: Jossey-Bass.

Pavakanun, U. and D'Ydewalle, G. (1992) Watching foreign television programs and language learning. In F.L. Engel, D.G. Bouwhuis, T. Bosser, and D'Ydewalle, G. (eds) *Cognitive Modelling and Interactive Environments In Language Learning*. Heidelberg: Verlag Berlin.

Rivers, W.M. and Temperley, M.S. (1978) *A Practical Guide to the Teachings of English*. New York: Oxford University Press.

Scarcella, R.C. and Oxford, R.L. (1992) *The Tapestry of Language Learning: The Individual in the Communicative Classroom*. Boston, MA: Heinle and Heinle.

Spolsky, B. (1989) *Conditions for Second Language Learning: Introduction to a General Theory*. Oxford: Oxford University Press.

Stephens, T.M. (1992) *Social Skill in the Classroom* (second edition). Odessa, FL: Psychological Assessment Resources.

Wallerstein, N. (1983) *Language and Culture in Conflict: Problem-posing in the ESL Classroom*. Reading, MA: Addison-Wesley.

Weltens, B., Van, E., Theo J.M. and Schils, E. (1989) The long-term retention of French by Dutch students. *Studies in Second Language Acquisition* 11 (2), 205–16.
Zich, P. (1986) *Teaching Ensemble Technique in Theatre*. London: International Schools Theatre Association.

7 Communicative Strategies for Intermediate Level Second Language Classes

SUZANNE MAJHANOVICH and JUMIN HU

Most recent language programmes claim to promote the communicative approach, and indeed many second language teachers also purport to teach communicatively. But what exactly is meant by communicative language teaching? Judging from programmes on the market, communicative language teaching can mean anything from modified audiolingualism to cognitive code teaching with an emphasis on context, to holistic language teaching through themes, an approach that seems to avoid the explicit presentation of language structures if at all possible.

The authors of this article are committed to second language practice that employs meaningful language used in context. They champion approaches that will develop communication strategies among students. At the same time, they also maintain with T. Higgs (1985) and Omaggio-Hadley (1993) that teaching communication strategies must always be balanced by attention to accuracy; indeed, one could argue that a message that is linguistically faulty may not, in fact, communicate the intended meaning.

Introduction

The notion of communicative competence as a goal of second or foreign language teaching has been around for over 20 years and has obviously had much influence on teaching approaches. Most recent language programmes claim to promote communicative language teaching, and indeed, many second language teachers purport to teach communicatively. The degree to which communicative activities actually drive second language instruction and the extent to which they can contribute to second language proficiency is less clear. There seems to be no doubt however, that communicative teaching when used judiciously and appropriately has made a major contribution to language teaching. To that end, this paper will review briefly some key studies in which communicative teaching was used, noting advantages and disadvantages. Then, a number of strategies are included which should promote communicative competence without neglecting attention to accuracy. The strategies, geared mainly to intermediate level students, entail to various extents the four language skills, and include as objectives the performance of typical communicative functions such as the development of:

- interpersonal skills through oral interviews;
- negotiation with an interlocutor to solve a problem and come to an agreement on an issue;
- expressive writing skills through personal and dialogue journals;
- the ability to converse logically and critically and defend a point of view in a debate.

We are committed to second language practice that employs meaningful language in context, and hence champion approaches that will develop communication strategies among students. At the same time, we believe, with Higgs & Clifford (1982), T.V. Higgs (1985) and A. Omaggio-Hadley (1993), that teaching communicative strategies must always be balanced by attention to accuracy. Indeed, one could argue that a message that is linguistically faulty may not, in fact, communicate the intended message. With that in mind, we will turn to a review of some studies which employed elements of communicative teaching and the conclusions drawn from those studies.

Development of the Concept and some Key Studies

In the early 1970s, Campbell and Wales (1970), commenting on Chomsky's competence-performance dichotomy, noted that Chomsky had omitted to include context in which language production occurs as a significant factor, and posited the idea that appropriateness of utterances within a situation was perhaps more indicative of a communication act than gramaticality *per se*. D. Hymes (1972) also theorised about a concept he called 'communicative competence' which incorporated not only grammatical competence but an awareness of appropriate socio-linguistic and contextual factors (See Omaggio-Hadley, 1993). Hence, the term 'communicative competence' came into the literature.

However, it was probably the work of Sandra Savignon, begun at the University of Illinois in the 1970s and described in *Communicative Competence: Theory and Classroom Practice* (1983) that really laid the groundwork for texts oriented toward communicative language teaching. Standard language classes never seemed to be able to deliver all they promised: depending on the approach used, students would learn grammar rules, or certain habits but could not use their language to communicate with others. Savignon theorised that students could be trained how to perform certain communicative acts. In the Illinois experiment, beginning college French classes were divided into three groups. For four of five scheduled classes per week, all three groups followed the regular programme using the assigned text. On the fifth day, however, the groups had different activities: one group went to the language laboratory for the usual drill and practice; a second group experienced a series of cultural sessions conducted in English including among others discussions about social, political and economic conditions in France, slides of French art and architecture, and informal meetings with French exchange students and Americans who had studied in France. The third group received instructions on how to perform a number of communicative functions in French such as greetings and leave taking, information getting and giving, providing description, and so on. Their sessions were made as relaxed and non-threatening as possible and students were encouraged to communicate their message any way they could. At the end of the 18-week session when all groups were tested, it was found that the linguistic competence among the three groups was roughly equal; however, the group that had practised communicative functions clearly surpassed the other two groups in communicative competence. Obviously, as with other skills, one learns to communicate by communicating. Savignon concluded that expressly communicative activities should become a part of second language classes if we want students to be able to communicate in their second language.

Despite the fact that the communicative aspect of the experiment comprised only 20% of the programme, the rest being devoted to the usual attention to form, nevertheless, the idea of communicative competence somehow became associated with getting meaning across without concern for grammatical accuracy. Savignon's definition of communicative competence stresses 'negotiation of meaning' however that may occur. Obviously, the ability to use circumlocution, mime or diagrams might be part of the negotiation. The problem, as pointed out by Higgs and Clifford (1982), Higgs (1985) is that Savignon's definition fails to take into account exactly *what* the student can communicate and *how well*. In other words, it is one thing to be able to communicate basic survival needs and quite another to negotiate, for example, an economic treaty.

Higgs and Clifford are concerned that when communicative competence comes to mean that one is to communicate the message in any possible way even in spite of language, then grammatical accuracy is overlooked. They prefer to view proficiency as the organising principle as evidenced in the Foreign Service Institute's proficiency ratings. These ratings include functions, content, and accuracy as components which are taken into consideration when evaluating competence in a foreign language on a scale from 0 to 5, where level 0 represents no functional ability to communicate while level 5 would equate with the ability of an educated native speaker. They profile the case of 'terminal 2/2+ students who seem to plateau at this level (apparently an all-too-common occurrence). Terminal 2/2+ students are understandable to most native speakers of the target language but lack the linguistic skills necessary to qualify them for most employment in which fluency in the target language is required. What seems to characterise a terminal 2 student is high vocabulary and fluency of a glib nature but fossilised grammatical patterns that are totally resistant to remediation. Such people have either acquired their language in an unstructured environment, on the streets as it were, in which case they might even be a terminal 1/1+, or if they have learned the language in an academic setting, it was either from a teacher who lacked competence in the language or in a programme which stressed communication by focusing on the message and not the form, and where errors were not corrected. Higgs and Clifford are adamant that their findings do not suggest a return to grammar-translation or audiolingual methodologies. They applaud techniques which encourage communication; they simply caution that if the communication demands placed on students greatly surpass the actual proficiency, they will be forced to resort to strategies which may lead to fossilisation. They conclude:

> ... it is meaningless to declare a student communicatively competent without specifying the language functions that he or she is competent to communicate [and] it is meaningless to declare any situation a communicative setting. A situation is a useful communicative setting only when the language functions it elicits are appropriate to the performance levels of the students (Higgs and Clifford, 1982: 78).

By suggesting that communicative competence included grammatical, discourse and sociolinguistic components, Canale (1983) made a valuable contribution to the definition of the concept. As a result, some important studies which measured the extent to which students could communicate effectively incorporating the three elements, as reported in Cummins and Swain (1986) and Allen, Swain *et al.* (1990) were carried out. In one study, Swain (Cummins & Swain, 1986) compared Grade 6 early immersion students to francophone counterparts and found that whereas there were minimal differences between the two groups with regard to discourse tasks, the native speakers performed significantly better on grammar tasks. Their advantage in grammatical competence also led them to outperform immersion students on sociological tasks where grammar was a factor as in cases which would require the use of the conditional. Otherwise, with regard to socio-linguistic tasks, immersion students tended to perform as well as the native speakers. These results led Swain to theorise on the importance of comprehensible input (see Krashen, 1981) for immersion students' acquisition of the language. While the input students had received in the programme led them to a high level of comprehension, it was insufficient to aid them in all communicative tasks. The massive input allowed students to comprehend by focusing on meaning without attending overtly to form. In order to enable students to better language production, Swain suggests that more comprehensible *output* be incorporated into the programme. Observations have convinced her that:

> students are not given... adequate opportunities to use the target language in the classroom context. Secondly, they are not 'pushed' in their output....There is no push for them to analyze further the grammar of the target language because their current output appears to succeed in conveying their intended message (Cummins & Swain, 1986: 133).

She concludes that immersion classes should provide more opportunities for comprehensible output where meaning is negotiated since within the contextualised meaningful exchanges, students, in order to negotiate meaning would be forced to test hypotheses about language and move beyond semantic analysis to syntactic analysis. This, she contends, would push students to acquire the grammatical competence they now lack.

In an expanded study on the development of bilingual proficiency reported in Harley, Allen *et al.* (1990), Swain and her researchers devised a scheme to measure what they called COLT (Communicative Orientation of Language Teaching). In that study, the researchers looked at core, extended and immersion as well as ESL classes. They predicted that the core French programmes because of their nature and time restraints would be more form-focused and teacher-centred (analytical or formal) than either the extended or immersion classes which would be less structured and more meaning-focused (experiential and functional). ESL classes, they thought, would incorporate authentic communicative materials from the surrounding milieu while focusing at the same time on certain aspects of the language code. Their expectations about the respective programmes were largely borne out; that is, the core French programmes were the most analytical and the immersion classes the most experiential, with the ESL classes falling somewhere between the others. This was an interesting case since it was ESL students who potentially had the greatest opportunity to profit from the environment outside the classroom to aid in language acquisition.

Swain concludes that analytical and experiential teaching can be complementary to SL programmes. Whereas core French programmes could benefit from more experiential teaching, immersion classes should definitely incorporate more chances for 'comprehensible output'. As she states: 'students need to be motivated to use language accurately, appropriately, and coherently' (Harley, Allen *et al.*, 1990: 77). Moreover, SL classes should provide situations where form and function would be closely linked instructionally. We take this to be in keeping with the caveats about communicative teaching as expressed by Higgs, Clifford and Omaggio.

We will now turn to some practical suggestions for communicative activities. They are geared mainly for students at the intermediate level or thereabouts. We believe that they all provide opportunities for 'comprehensible output', but they are devised in such a way as not to put excessive communicative demands on the students' language competence.

Strategies for a Communicative Classroom

Classroom Strategy 1

Title: Peer Interview. (Questionnaire)
Objective: To develop interpersonal oral communication skills
Context: Personal life, experiences, opinions, etc.
Procedure: Design a questionnaire that contains a number of simple questions likely to be relevant to the students. Distribute copies of the questionnaire to each member of the class (or two groups if the class is large). Go over all the unfamiliar words in the questionnaire. Then have students interview one another within the class/group in a courteous manner. The interviewer jots down the appropriate answer from the interviewee as well as the answer to at least one follow-up question related to the first answer. The student who first solicits appropriate answers to all or the largest number of the questions in a given time wins first place. Students gather in small groups to share their answers.

Example: Interview your peers and find one answer to each of the following questions. Ask an additional question to obtain further information.

(1) Who was born in December?

(2) Who plays a musical instrument?

(3) Who had a nightmare last night?

(4) Who walks to school every day?

(5) Who usually gets up at 6.30 in the morning?

(6) Who lives in a townhouse?

(7) Whose father is a doctor?

(8) Who knows someone from Montreal?

(9) Who has been to the United States?/to Europe/Asia, etc.

(10) Who does not have a driving licence?

(11) Who is particularly fond of Italian food?

(12) Who likes to work on computers?

Comments: The questions should be so designed that students may find answers to most or all of them. For advanced students, questions that require more elaborate answers can be substituted. The questions in the format above can be answered as the students supply factual information about themselves and therefore can be called an 'uncontrolled peer interview'. This interview works well with students who are still in the process of getting to know one another. However, for students already well acquainted with each other, the teacher may wish to use prepared cards and have students answer the questions according to the information shown on his/her card given by the teacher. This format may be called a 'controlled peer interview'. Alternatively, students could list questions they would like to ask of their classmates. To attend to accuracy, when students share their answers in small groups, they should be encouraged to ask for clarification if the answer is not clear or incorrect (peer correction).

Classroom Strategy 2

Title: Problem-Solving Conversation.
Objective: To negotiate with the interlocutor in order to work out a solution to or agreement on a problem.
Context: Everyday social situations
Procedure: Create a problem and present it on cards A and B to be solved through conversation between two students, who may need to play certain social roles. In order to reach a solution or agreement, the two interlocutors have to exchange information supplied on their separate cards and negotiate toward various possibilities of settlement. After the first round of conversation, the two students exchange their cards and switch roles for a second round.

Example:

A. Prospective Tenant   **B.** Landlord

Call to inquire if B has a room   Answer the call; say you have one for
for rent.   rent.

Ask about location, room size,   Give details of location, room size and
facilities.   facilities.

Ask about rent and terms of   Quote a price e.g. $350./mo., 12-month
lease.   lease

Tell B you have your own   Agree to A's offer on condition that A
furniture.   pays for utilities/Disagree; make a
                                   counter offer.

Make an offer to pay a lower
amount/mo.

Accept B's conditions/Bargain further.

Comments: The problem topics should be relevant to the students' concerns or within the students' scope of interest. In all cases, the difficulty and complexity level of the conversation should be adjusted to suit the specific groups of students. Difficult key words can be glossed at the bottom of the cards. The teacher circulates among the groups, offering help to needy students. Once a pair is done with a problem, they pass it to the next pair while another problem is passed to them. The teacher controls the flow of problems according to the time planned for the activity. This strategy is somewhat similar to the role play element of the ACTFL Proficiency Interview (ACTFL, 1989). Near the end of the interview, when the interviewer has established what appears to be the proficiency level of the interviewee (intermediate, advanced or superior) he/she hands the inter- viewee a card which gives a situation to be acted out. The intermediate level cards include features which will check the interviewee's ability to create with language, ask and answer simple questions and handle a simple situation or transaction. Advanced level role plays include opportunities to narrate, describe and handle a complicated situation or transaction, while superior role plays push the interviewee to support opinions, hypothesise, discuss abstract topics and handle linguistically unfamiliar situations. Performance is judged on content, accuracy, and functions including discourse, sociolinguistic and pragmatic competence. An excellent source of role play situations can also be found in Stephen Sadow's book, *Idea Bank: Creative Activities for the Language Class* (1982).

Classroom Strategy 3

Title: Journal Dialogue.
Objective: To develop expressive writing skills in meaningful ways.
Context: Areas of interest or concern to individual students.
Procedure: Ask students to write a journal once or twice a week as part of their homework. To make the experience personally meaningful, students are free to write on/about anything that is interesting, relevant, and/or significant to them, from personal emotions and concerns to political issues to intellectual explorations. Some journal writing may involve pre-reading of publications and references. Although in principle no limit should be set for how long a journal should be, one page can be a realistic goal for intermediate students to start with. Students are encouraged to express their thoughts as freely as they wish. The teacher collects the journals, reads them, and responds with an entry of comments and/or questions. The students may or may not choose to respond to the teacher's entry. If he/she does (as often happens), a second response follows (then a third, etc.), thus creating a journal dialogue between teacher and student.

Example: No examples are provided for this strategy, since journals are typically personal.

Comments. The Journal Dialogue can provide not only for linguistic but also emotional or intellectual development. In order to direct students toward high language proficiency, the teacher should encourage students to aim at accuracy as well as expressiveness. In addition to commenting on the content, the teacher should correct grammar, rhetorical and typographical errors. But if the journal contains too many such errors, the teacher may correct the most serious mistakes only in the initial stage and gradually take care of the others. Students at basic levels may write about their family, everyday life, and the like. The journal can be as long as a few sentences. However, for advanced students, more complicated topics, greater journal length, and more accuracy can be expected.

Classroom Strategy 4

Title: Debate.
Objective: To train students to think logically and critically.
Context: Topics/situations of common concern

Procedure: Divide students into groups of three to five. Assign a pro-position on a common question/topic/issue to Group A and a counter-position to Group B. After a brief intra-group discussion which involves brainstorming to generate key arguments, the two groups debate the issue. Group A presents its position and arguments; Group B attacks Group A, supplying its own arguments and position. Group A fires back, and so on. A conclusion may or may not be reached. Each group can be represented by one or more spokespersons.

Example: The North American Free Trade Agreement (NAFTA) Group A—Supporters; Group **B**—Critics.

A: NAFTA gives Canadian companies a bigger market. They can sell their products in Mexico. This means more jobs in Canada.

B: Canada will lose jobs. Wages are very low in Mexico. Industries that need a lot of labour will move south. Some examples are auto parts and furniture.

A: Companies will stay here. Canada has advantages such as good technology and skilled workers.

B: Companies will also move because Mexico does not have strong environmental, health and safety laws. Production costs are lower.

A: The North American Free Trade Agreement is building for the future. We might lose some jobs as Canada adjusts to free trade, but our economy will benefit in the long term.

B: We are trading away our future. Canada is losing its competitive advantage and control over its economy. There will be more advantages for companies to invest in the United States or Mexico.

   Source: Adapted from 'North American Free Trade: Opinion divided, *The Ontario Times* (October 1992), p. 2.

Comments: Alternatively, students could read a short passage on a provocative topic as, for example, progress in medicine or advantages and disadvantages of various media. In whole class discussion, they enlarge on the topic and then in groups prepare a list of pros and cons on the issue and finally debate it. As a follow-up activity, they might be asked to prepare a written composition on the topic. See Majhanovich and Willis (1984) *Ça y est Question à débattre* in each unit. To prepare students for the discourse elements required to support and refute arguments, teachers could provide the necessary vocabulary beforehand including words and expressions such as: 'on the one hand', 'on the other hand', 'however', 'nevertheless', 'despite all', 'let's admit that...', 'after all', and so on if students are not familiar with these words. Discourse competence often lies not merely in a sense of how to discuss something cohesively, or in an appropriate order: most SL learners can transfer this from their first language experiences. What they lack is the vocabulary necessary to link their statements. It would seem appropriate for teachers to spend some time providing the necessary linking words and encouraging students to pay attention to them and use them appropriately in oral and written communication. Regarding topics, generally, intermediate students would feel comfortable with survival topics related to everyday life such as living, recreation and health matters; whereas advanced students would find it interesting to challenge topics concerning education, politics, economics, culture, moral issues and so on. But some questions of the latter category can be discussed by intermediate university students, given limited complexity and duration of the debate. If necessary, extra information on content, sentence structure and vocabulary can be provided by the teacher beforehand. The same ques-tions/topics/issues can be circulated to different groups at varying times. All students speak in the target language. While the debates go on, the teacher moves around participating or helping students with difficult expressions. Each session takes 20–30 minutes.

Summary

This chapter has discussed the development of the concept of commu-nicative competence and reviewed a number of key studies in which communicative activities or teaching played a role. We repeat that we believe that strategies which will promote communicative competence should be promoted in second language classes. We also are aware of the inherent dangers of encouraging communication for its own sake without attention to accuracy and the proficiency level of the students. Hence, the strategies we have suggested, while communicative, are controlled to a certain extent so that the SL learners while experimenting with and testing their hypotheses about language will not be forced into communicative situations too far removed form their actual level.

Students almost always underestimate the time and commitment needed to acquire a second language; teachers are perhaps too optimistic in their expectation for their students as well. Nevertheless, with a well-rounded programme that pays attention to content, functions and accuracy, a bank of activities that will address the students' needs at every level of proficiency, and sufficient time to achieve the objectives, the goal of competent communicators in the SL should be realisable.

References

Allen, J.P.B., Swain, M., Harley, B. and Cummins, J. (1990) Aspects of classroom treatment: Toward a more comprehensive view of second language education. In B. Harley, P. Allen, J. Cummins and M. Swain (eds) *The Development of Second Language Proficiency*. Cambridge: Cambridge University Press.

Buck, K., Byrnes, H. and Thompson, I. (eds) (1989) *The ACTFL Oral Proficiency Interview*. Yonkers, NY: American Council on the Teaching of Foreign Languages.

Campbell, R. and Wales, R. (1970) The study of language acquisition. In J. Lyons (ed.) *New Horizons in Linguistics*. Harmondsworth, England: Penguin Books.

Canale, M. (1983) From communicative competence to communicative language pedagogy. In J. Richards and R. Schmidt (eds) *Language and Communication*. London: Longman Group.

Cummins, J. and Swain, M. (1986) Communicative competence: Some roles of comprehensible input and comprehensible output in its development. In J. Cummins and M. Swain (eds) *Bilingual Education*. New York: Longman Group Ltd.

Higgs, T.V. (ed.) (1985) *Teaching for Proficiency, the Organizing Principle*. The ACTFL Foreign Language Education Series, Vol 15. Lincolnwood, IL: National Textbook Co.

Higgs, T.V. and Clifford, R. (1982) The push toward communication. In T.V. Higgs (ed.) *Curriculum Competence and the Foreign Language Teacher*. The ACTFL Foreign Language Education Series, Vol. 13, Lincolnwood, IL: National Textbook Co.

Hymes, D. (1972) On communicative competence. In J.B. Pride and J. Holmes (eds) *Sociolinguistics*. Harmondsworth, England: Penguin Books.

Krashen, S. (1981) *Second Language Acquisition and Second Language Learning*. Oxford: Pergamon.

Majhanovich, S. and Willis, P. Wahl. (1984) *Ça y est!* Toronto: Copp Clark Pitman.

Omaggio-Hadley, A. (1993) *Teaching Language in Context* (2nd edition). Boston, MA: Heinle & Heinle.

Sadow, S.A. (1982) *Idea Bank: Creative Activities for the Language Class*. Rowley, MA: Newbury House.

Savignon, S.J. (1983) *Communicative Competence: Theory and Classroom Practice*. Reading, MA: Addison-Wesley.

8 Magic or Chaos: Task-based Group Work

CHRISTINA BRATT PAULSTON and GAIL BRITANIK

This chapter discusses taskbased group work from a practical, classroom-oriented perspective. After a brief consideration of the pedagogical reasons and theoretical psycholinguistic rationales for group work, we consider basic procedures and strategies for conducting group work. The chapter closes with five classroom activities in which basic procedures discussed earlier are specified for each activity as exemplars of what to consider in creating and conducting group work.

Educational practice shows a continual tendency to oscillate between two extremes with respect to two overt and executive activities. One extreme is to neglect them always entirely, on the grounds that they are chaotic and fluctuating, mere diversions... The other extreme is an enthusiastic belief in the almost magical educative efficacy of any activity... (John Dewey (1910), cited in Bygate, 1992).

While ESL teachers seem to be imbued with the magical view of the efficacy of group work, 'the most serious of all problems is ignored: that of discovering and arranging the forms of activity... which are most congenial, best adapted to the... stage of development' (Dewey, 1910). That, quite simply, is what this chapter is about.

Kenneth Pike is reported to have said that classroom teachers know what it will take linguists decades to discover. A good example of that is group work. Second language acquisition (SLA) linguists are now discovering theoretical, i.e. psycholinguistic, rationales for doing group work. We have long known the pedagogical reasons for doing group work. Long and Porter (1985) list: (1) increasing the quantity of language practice opportunity; (2) improving the quality of student talk; (3) creating a positive affective climate in the classroom; (4) individualising instruction; and (5) increasing student motivation. Porter and Danielson (1991) say almost the same thing: (1) students get more practice; (2) students use a wider range of language; (3) more individualized instruction is possible; (4) it promotes a positive affective climate; (5) it motivates learners and (6) it provides variety in the classroom. They add that students say that (1) they like sharing and exchanging ideas; (2) it leads to more learning, understanding, and practice; and (3) it motivates them.

Mary McGroarty suggests an unusual benefit, namely that cooperative learning provides an opportunity for use of the first language in ways that support cognitive development as well as increased second language skills. She cites a study on elementary school children (Neves, 1983) and speculates that:

> academic use of the primary language helps students master English, perhaps by consolidating their conceptual knowledge in settings that allow them to use the first language while being exposed to appropriate second language labels naturally during groupwork (McGroarty, 1989: 133).

Teacher criticism of group work, the chaos view, centres on waste of time, too time consuming, general confusion and only a few of the students doing the work. While there is often justification for these criticisms, in view of the importance of the theoretical claims made for the crucial necessity of group work, those problems can be dealt with procedurally, as we shall discuss. To claim as a teacher did, recently observed, that he had to cover nine (new) tenses in ESL in a one-hour class and so had no time for communicative activities is not teaching ESL; at best it is a linguistic lecture, hardly conducive to learning a second language.

The psycholinguistic claims for taskbased group work are basically three. They provide: (1) for comprehensible input (Krashen, 1980, Gass & Varonis, 1985); (2) for extended negotiation of meaning (Long, 1989); and (3) maybe most important, for comprehensible output (Swain, 1985). Classroom based SLA research over the last 15 years, such as that done by Pica and Doughty (1985), Doughty and Pica (1986), and Pica et al., (1987) point to the value of two-way over one-way tasks in generating negotiation of meaning, with an increase of almost 10 times the amount of interaction in group work over teacher-fronted class situations when interaction was *required*, rather than optional. This chapter is not the place for psycholinguistic speculations, but let us point out that these three types of language processing listed above are today held crucial for effective adult second language acquisition and it is simply false economy to talk about too time-consuming activities if without them the students won't learn as well. Instead we should worry about how group work can be 'most congenial, best adapted'.

What follows is a brief discussion of basic procedures and strategies for conducting group work. We acknowledge that teachers have different (and sometimes strong) opinions about some of these guidelines, and it is perfectly true that what works well for one class may not work in another. Underlying these guidelines is the need to keep an open mind and to use a principled trial-and-error approach. Such an approach includes constant objective evaluation of all activities in terms of their contribution to students' learning and a willingness to see occasional failures as a normal part of doing group work.

Pre-class Preparation

The first step is to decide on performance objectives. Using an activity without a specific pedagogical aim is most often a waste of time. The objectives may vary from form-focused practice, such as questions on likes and dislikes (see Activity 1 'Find someone who... '), to general language use in the production of some tasks like the class booklet (see Activity 4); but in both activities the teacher knows what s/he wants to achieve. This really is a crucial step.

If you are lucky, your textbook will include group activities. If not, get your institution to invest in a collection of texts aimed at group work, like *Using English, Your Second Language* or *Strategic Interaction* from which you can collect and adapt activities. What is important is that the task is at the right level of students' proficiency. Classroom pre-activities can do much to help, especially with vocabulary and content knowledge for context. Some general recommendations for task structure are (Long, 1989; Porter and Danielson, 1991): (i) include a brief (2–3 minutes) planning time before the activity during which students individually can consider their plan of attack; (ii) tasks which have two-way structure produce more negotiation, i.e. tasks where both/all students in a group must exchange information such as in Activity 3 'Travellers' advice' where each student is an 'expert' and has information unknown to the others, and in Activity 4 'Creating a Class Booklet' where there is some shared information but also information exclusive to each role. One-way information gap activities in which one partner has all the information while the other takes directions in order to draw a picture or plot a route on a map, etc. generate less negotiation since the *exchange* of information is optional; (iii) closed tasks (Long's terminology) also produce more negotiation; i.e. a task which has only one or two correct solutions. Keep in mind the point Pica and Doughty make:

> However, group work alone does not appear to be an affective aid to classroom learning. Rather, what seems essential is the combination of

group interaction and a task requiring the exchange of information among group participants (1988:54).

In Class Pre-activity

Divide the class quickly into groups and establish procedures for doing so which are always followed, such as students wait to move until the teacher gives the sign, they leave their books on their desks or bring them along, etc. What you want to vary is the composition of the groups, which should be kept small. You will want to consider such factors as level of proficiency, talkativeness, shyness, language background, age, etc. There are different opinions on pairing all of these, so our suggestion is that you try different combinations to see what works best in your classroom. But here are a few suggestions: keep the groups small with no more than three or four students in a group; don't have a group of all the same language background (with adult students, it does not contradict McGroarty) if possible, and make sure there is at least one strong student in each group.

You may want some preparation time for the students, to work on vocabulary, grammar patterns, or culture specific ways with language according to the performance objectives. Knowing a task is coming up, students are always highly motivated to work hard in this situation.

Activity

Set time limitations and don't give them too much time; it is not always necessary to have all groups finish a task. Make sure the early finishers have something to do and don't just sit there. The teacher should circulate around the room, checking that the students are on track, be willing to answer questions, and helping out in general. Provide for some sort of closure to the activity, like having one group report back to the class, but keep this brief; the students have already done the activity and reports easily become boring. Another type of closure is to have groups with different solutions to the same task argue their point. Teacher ingenuity will think up other possibilities, but however brief, psychologically there is a need for closure so don't just finish with 'Time's up, goodbye'.

Feedback and/or Evaluation

It is a good idea to have each group turn in something tangible to the teacher after the activity. It keeps the students task-oriented, gives information to the teacher about how well the activity worked, and is something to base feedback on. It is also a good idea to have the students rate the activity. If they find all activities boring, something is wrong. And they can have quite insightful remarks about procedures as well.

And as a final evaluation ask yourself: 'Could the students just as well have done this group work in McDonald's?' If an honest answer is in the affirmative (and sometimes it is), we suggest you rethink the magic of taskbased group work in terms of 'educative efficacy'.

What follows are five activities which exemplify the principles and procedures we have been discussing. They are designed to give you maximum guidance as you introduce your class to group work.

Activity 1   Signature activity: 'Find someone who… '

Proficiency Level: Intermediate.

Performance Objectives: Asking questions, giving answers, and stating preferences (This may be altered to meet other objectives. See below.)

Teacher Preparation: Prepare an activity sheet, listing possible favorite activities or interests. (See below.) To personalise the activity you might include the items students had mentioned on a registration form or during an interview in response to a question about their interests or hobbies.

Include these written directions:

> Read the list of 15 items below. Think of the question you will need to ask to find someone who agrees with the item. For example, to find someone who likes cooking, you would ask, 'Do you like to cook?' When you find that person ask her/him to sign her/his name on the line after that item. Try to find a different person for each item.

Prepare enough copies for the entire class.

Pre-activity: Review verbs used to express preference. Give an example: ('I enjoy taking long walks.') Write on the chalkboard or overhead projector: *prefer, like, enjoy, dislike, detest, hate.* Offer another example ('I dislike cold weather.') Explain or review degrees of intensity expressed by dislike, detest, hate. Ask a student to state a preference. Ask another to use dislike in a sentence.

Distribute copies of activity sheet to each student. Ask students to read the directions silently. When they have finished, use the first item to model the procedure. Ask a student, 'Do you enjoy cooking?' If the student responds: 'Yes, I enjoy cooking', ask him to write his signature in the appropriate space on your paper. If he says: 'No', move on to another student. Ask students if they understand what to do. Say: 'You will have about 10 minutes to find all the signatures you need.' Try to get a different person's signature for each item. Call for an end to the activity when several students have acquired signatures for most of the items on the list. If the class seems to need more time, adjust the time allotment.

Activity: Students move around the room asking questions of one another and giving answers.

Signature activity

Find someone who: Signature

(1) enjoys mystery films   _____
(2) dislikes eating ice cream   _____
(3) likes loud music   _____
(4) enjoys swimming or playing tennis   _____
(5) detests cigarette smoke   _____
(6) prefers reading to watching television   _____
(7) likes to eat pizza   _____
(8) dislikes shopping malls   _____
(9) likes to play the guitar or piano   _____
(10) prefers Rock music to Bach   _____
(11) enjoys eating in a restaurant   _____
(12) hates cold weather   _____
(13) prefers cats to dogs   _____
(14) likes to fly in an airplane   _____
(15) prefers climbing mountains to watching
    television   _____

Post Activity: After seven minutes check to see how many have finished. Tell students they have a few minutes to finish. Then ask a student: 'Who did you find who likes to play the guitar or piano?' Did anyone else find a musician? Ask: 'Which was the most difficult to find? Which was the easiest? For homework, think of the verbs we've used (*prefer, like, enjoy, dislike, detest, hate*) and use those verbs to make up five interesting questions you would like to ask. You will have the opportunity to use those questions during our next class.'

Adaptation: This activity could be used early in the semester to help students get to know each other as well as to give practice in asking questions and giving answers. For example: 'Find someone who knows three others in the class, who has travelled to New York (Tokyo, Toronto, Paris, etc.)', etc.

Other possible adaptations: *Review of a thematic unit*, for example, on food. Questions could include: 'Find someone who doesn't like to eat meat;

enjoys growing her own vegetables; prefers fruit to pastries, etc.' *A fact check on a content based unit, e.g. a international trade unit which could include items such as: Find someone who knows what the main exports of _____ are; which areas of the world are famous for _____, etc.' *Practice of Verb tenses e.g.; 'Find someone who worked as a teacher in her native country; someone who built houses; etc.

Activity 2 Dining guide: Making choices

Proficiency Level: Intermediate.

Performance Objectives: Listening to the preferences of others, negotiating to arrive at a consensus; and practising skimming and scanning.

Teacher Preparation: Use this activity as a follow-up to a unit on food, meals, dining at home or in a restaurant. Select the 'Dining Guide' from a local newspaper or clip restaurant advertisements from newspapers and assemble a dining guide offering a diversity of cuisine, price, location and entertainment options, etc. Make copies for each student. Prepare a graphic organiser for use on the overhead projector to record class brainstorming results. Prepare cards or sheets of paper posing three problems/activities for group decision. (See directions below.)

Pre-Activity: To the whole group pose the question: 'Do you ever go out to eat in a restaurant? How do you decide which restaurant to choose? Use an overhead projection, 'Choosing a restaurant: Things to consider'). Elicit the following information from students:

What things do you consider when choosing a place to eat?
Type of food: Italian, Chinese, Mid-Eastern, Mexican, American, etc. *Kind of restaurant*: fast food, diner, cafe, formal, deli, bar, etc. *Price range*: expensive, moderate, inexpensive. *Atmosphere*: quiet, noisy, hurried, friendly, relaxed, smoke filled, etc. *Location*: in walking distance from home, on a busline, near the university, etc.

Ask about additional considerations, e.g.: Is there entertainment in the evenings? Is the restaurant open seven days a week? Are any of these restaurants 'handicapped accessible?' (Clarify the meaning. Explain, if necessary, that more places are offering elevators or ramps for access to those who have difficulty walking stairs.) Discuss other considerations.

---

*Adapted from *Keep Talking* by Friederike Klippel, Cambridge University Press (1984) and observation of a class taught by Dr Richard Donato, January 1993 at the University of Pittsburgh.

Activity: Distribute copies of the 'Dining Guide'. Ask students to skim the listings and think about which places seem most attractive to them. Ask students to check off three places where they might like to eat. Ask: 'Where can you find Italian food? Which restaurant is most expensive? How do you know?' (Make sure students understand the code: $$$, $$, $ and indications of which, if any, credit cards are acceptable.). Ask students to form groups of three and to discuss the restaurants they are interested in for a few minutes. As students are forming groups distribute cards with the following problems for solution:

(1) Agree on one restaurant where you three will eat tonight.

(2) Select a restaurant where you will celebrate a friend's birthday. Remember, this friend detests smoking. You have a limited amount of money to spend.

(3) Find a restaurant that would be a good place to go with a friend for a quiet conversation. The friend does not eat meat.

Circulate among groups, reminding students that everyone in each group must be satisfied with the choices made. (Limit the discussion and choice-making to 10–12 minutes.) Ask groups to end their discussion and ask one group to report on their selection for (1). Ask another group to explain their choice for (2); another group for (3). Elicit students' response to the question, 'Which is easie-- to make your own choice independently or to find agreement among the three of you?' 'Why?'

For homework ask students to create an original (imaginary) restaurant advertisement to bring to class the following day. Use five minutes of the following class to have them exchange the ad with one other student and offer feedback to each other on the ad. Post the student-made ads on the class bulletin board.

Adaptations: Rather than the teacher preparing a dining guide, ask students to bring examples of restaurant ads from home, or have newspapers or the telephone book available for their use. Have students find a restaurant they would recommend to the class and explain why. Use a newspaper entertainment page to choose a film or musical or sports event that will meet the needs of everyone in the small group.

Source: Lesson plan designed for use with Adult ESL class by Gail Britank at the University of Pittsburgh, October 1992.

Activity 3   Travellers' advice

Proficiency Level: Intermediate/Advanced.

Performance Objectives: Making recommendations with supporting reasons and offering advice.

Teacher Preparation: Bring a world map to class. Prepare a student activity sheet (below): 'Travellers' Advice' which includes two sections:

(1) If you visit my country, I recommend that you go to_____ because: (List three reasons.) _____.
(2) Before I travelled to another country, I wish someone had told me: (List several things you wish you had known before travelling.) _____.

   (You may want to pre-determine the grouping to assure an international diversity.)

Pre-Activity: Display the world map. Invite students to locate their country for the class. Write 'TRAVEL' on the board and elicit vocabulary connected with the theme. (Means of transportation, visas, currency exchange, insurance, reservations, health concerns, etc.) Ask students to think about a special place in their countries which they have visited and would recommend to visitors. Distribute activity sheets and ask students to write the name of the place and think of two or three reasons why they would recommend this place.

Activity: Pair work: Assign students to work in pairs. Tell them that they will be listening to each other's recommendations. Later they will be responsible to tell others about their partners' favourite place. Students share in pairs. (five minutes) Then two pairs form a group of four and take turns reporting to the other pair what they learned from their partner, checking to make sure they've included all important information (eight minutes).

   Group work: Ask students to think of advice that would be important to potential travellers. Ask them: 'What do you wish someone had told you before you travelled to another country?' Have students take a few minutes to make their own lists, then take turns sharing with the others. Encourage students to ask for clarification as others speak. The group will complete the activity sheet, listing five or six things they would tell travelers prior to international travel. Tell students that these will be reported to the whole class during the next class period. (These results could be gathered into a booklet with their recommendations about favourite places in each of their countries with photos or illustrations later in the semester.)

Adaptations: (1) Change this to an interview activity during which students would work in pairs and then introduce their partners to the class telling about two or three things they learned during the exchange.

(2) Use this activity as a preparation for a visit from a travel agent who would give a brief presentation to the class and answer questions which students would prepare as a final part of this activity. 'Think of three questions you would like to ask a travel agent in this country before you travel again.'

Student activity sheet

PART I.

Directions: Think about a special place in your country that you have visited. You are going to tell your partner about that place and describe it as well as you can. Think of three reasons why you would recommend that place to someone who is planning to visit your country.

When you visit my country I recommend that you visit _____, located in the _____region.

Here are three reason why I'm recommending that you visit this place:

(1)

(2)

(3)

PART II.

After you listen to your partner give her/his recommendation about a special place, you will be responsible for telling two other people about your partner's recommendation. You can use this space to make notes to help you remember.

(1)

(2)

(3)

Source: Designed by Gail Britanik for use with adult ESL students, February 1993 at the University of Pittsburgh.

Part III.

Think about some problems you have had when you travelled to the United States or to other places.

Have you wished that someone had told you before you travelled what to expect or how to avoid problems?

Think of a few things that you wish someone had told you before you began a trip.

I wish that someone had told me:

(1)

(2)

(3)

Activity 4   Creating a class booklet

Level: Intermediate/Advanced.

Performance Objectives: Contributing efficiently at each phase of the group work process:

- Cooperative planning and design
- Peer interviews
- Writing and revising

Teacher Preparation: This task is an integrative one to be used toward the end of a semester. All preceding activities serve as preparation. As immediate preparation the teacher could bring booklets produced by other groups or simply make a mock-up of what such a booklet might look like. The booklet will include: a cover designed by the students; interviews of each member of the class written by students; some aspect of students' cultural heritage (a brief description of a holiday, a recipe, a poem or song, etc.) contributed by each student; and a photograph of each student. The role of the teacher is to present the project idea, elicit students' ideas, facilitate the process by organising students into working groups offering suggestions and asking clarifying questions as needed and assisting in final production (printing, etc.). Make arrangements for use of typewriters or computers for student use in production of booklets. Plan on four or five class periods to accomplish the project.

Pre-activity: Day One. Introduce the idea of a class booklet as a way to summarise the work of the semester, and to work together on a product they can keep to remember the class. Show students samples of booklets produced by other groups or a mock-up of what a booklet might look like. Ask students for ideas about what they want to put in their booklet. Offer suggestions if students need help to get started, writing all ideas on the chalkboard. If there are many ideas, you will probably need to ask students to select four or five categories of entries: interviews, photos, customs, recipes, etc. to make the project realisable.

Designing a work plan: Ask students to think about the jobs that need to be done to produce the booklet, eliciting responses, asking for clarification, and writing a list of 'jobs' on the chalkboard. If small (8–12 students), the class could be divided into two groups: *Writing* – those who will do interviews of all class members and coordinate proofreading and editing; and *Design* – those who will choose a title for the booklet, design the cover, collect photos, recipes and/or custom descriptions from each student, and do the layout for the booklet. (Larger classes could have tasks further divided: two writing groups, etc.)

Homework: Ask students in the writing group to make a list of possible interview questions they will ask their peers. They should be ready to share those questions in their group at the beginning of the following class. Ask those in the Design group to make a list of possible titles for the booklet and think about possible layout plans and graphics they might like to use. Ask them to look at magazines and newspapers to find possible pictures and graphics and bring these to class.

Activity: Day Two. Ask students to meet in work groups and share ideas they have and come to a consensus. The Design group will need to select a title from among the ideas they bring to class, possibly combining ideas. This process will generate conversation, negotiation and sometimes a bit of controversy. (The teacher would do well to allow students to deal with the problem, perhaps intervening with a clarifying question or a reminder that this must be a group decision and that there is a time limit.) The group should also decide on graphics and a general layout plan by the end of the period. They will need to talk with the writing group to request necessary materials (photos, a recipe, etc.) and ask that all materials be brought to the next class.

The Writing group will come to agreement on the questions to be used in the interview process and decide which two students each one will interview. They should begin by interviewing one another (in pairs) and making arrangements with students in the design group for interviews before the next class if possible. The teacher will need to remind students of the three or four paragraph length for interviews.

Before the end of the class period, ask students to report on their progress to the whole group. Ask them what work will be done outside of class and write those tasks on the chalkboard. Remind students about the time limitation and encourage them to complete the work before the next class. Check to see which students are able to help with data entry or typing. Offer assistance if any is needed.

Day Three. Ask students to get into work groups and share what they have accomplished. Design group asks Writing group for photos and recipes, etc. and begins to work on layout plan, allotting one or one-and-a-half pages for each student feature.

The Writing group confers with one another in pairs reading the text of the interviews and asking for clarification, checking for accuracy and making suggestions. The teacher is available to answer questions, and help with editing.

After 20 minutes members of the Writing group meet with those they interviewed from the Design group to check for accuracy, etc. The teacher uses the last 10–15 minutes of the period to coordinate final layout and make arrangements for typing or computer entry of final draft, making copies. Tell students that the following class period will be used to collate the booklets and to read and discuss it.

Day Four. Help students set up a system to collate the pages to assemble the booklet. (This can be done in 15 minutes.) Use the remaining time to allow students to read the booklet and make comments. Ask students: 'What was good about the class booklet project? What did you learn? What was most difficult? What could have been done better?'

Adaptation: The booklet could be planned over a longer period of time, perhaps beginning half way through the semester and developed over a course of four to six weeks, using one class period each week to work toward the final product. The interviews could be done as part of a re-writing project based on earlier class interviews and increased in length and improved grammar usage. The inclusion of cultural heritage could grow out of a unit on international diversity. A page on 'Highlights' of the semester could be added as the result of a class brainstorming session about world and local events, films and music they know and enjoy and class activities and progress. Booklets could be produced on a variety of topics that reflect content based instruction.

Source: This project plan is based on my observation of an Adult ESL class taught by Janis Scalone, November 1992, and was expanded upon during work with a group of high intermediate students whom I taught in the spring of 1993 at the University of Pittsburgh. (G.B.)

Activity 5   Community problems and solutions: Interactive field trip

Requires three class periods.

Performance Objectives: Interacting with persons beyond the classroom, asking for information, listening and checking for comprehension.

Proficiency Level: Intermediate/Advanced.

Teacher Preparation: This activity requires long-range planning by the teaching staff. However, once the outreach into the community has been accomplished, the structure will be in place for future classes on an annual basis. The activity expands the classroom walls outward into the local community and puts students in touch with community services – bank, food cooperative or buying club, hospital or health clinic, the local police or public safety centre, newspaper, library or museum.

Choose a site of interest to students. (This can be done by having students indicate their interests on a simple questionnaire that lists agencies, businesses and community organisations. Have students work in pairs, then groups of four to prioritise their interests). (1) Call or write a letter to the public service or community outreach personnel, inquiring about the possibility of a field trip to their agency. Explain the goals of the ESL project, the time that the class meets, the number of students, the student proficiency level and suggest a format for the visit. If appropriate, ask for an appointment for further discussion and to make specific arrangements. Ask that an agency representative meet with the students to explain the purpose and work of the agency, give a tour of the facility, if possible, and then answer questions which students will have prepared prior to the visit. Explain that the field trip is part of a unit dealing with community services and that students will be studying vocabulary, preparing questions and will be accompanied by the instructor. If the public service representative agrees to host the class, schedule the visit a month in advance, ask for informational brochures that could be used as part of the preparation and arrange to call the representative a week prior to the field trip to confirm plans. (If you plan to videotape or audiotape the session, ask permission in advance. The taped portion of the visit will focus on students' interaction with the personnel and be used for evaluation and future planning by students and teachers.) If the community relations director seems interested but is unable to have the class visit the facility, ask if s/he or a representative would be available to visit the class to explain services. Collect posters and pictures, brochures, magazine ads and articles related to the topic you have chosen for a classroom display. For example, if the topic is health care, collect posters advertising health services, immunisation campaigns, health education programmes, nutrition and vitamins, etc.

(You may want to ask students to keep a special section of their notebooks for this community field trip unit. Students can record new vocabulary, questions they have about the topic and reflections and evaluation after the field trip.)

Pre-activity: Day One. Introduce the topic; explain that the class will be investigating some services in the community. List : health care, safe neighbourhoods, fresh food markets, banking, newspaper, museum, etc. on the chalkboard. Explain that arrangements have been made for the class to visit some of these facilities during the semester and that we will begin with a visit to a nearby hospital at the end of the week.

Distribute pictures and posters depicting health care needs/provisions/concerns/vitamin advertisements, pictures of children being immunised, nutritional posters, pictures of nurses, doctors, patients, healthy looking people walking, playing ball, etc. Ask students to examine the pictures. Include brochures from the local hospital.

Write the word, 'HEALTH' on an overhead projector. Ask students to think of words that come to mind when they hear this word. Write responses on the chart. Ask what is the opposite of health? Record responses on the overhead. Ask students to think of a time when someone in their family was ill. What happened? How was the family member cared for? Did a doctor care for the person? If students have not had such an experience, ask them to think about what they would do if a family member got sick while they were living here in the US. As students are considering these points direct them to find a partner to work with. Begin with brainstorming. (As students are brainstorming, the teacher walks among the group listening, offering help as needed, taking note of vocabulary that is being used or is needed. Write the vocabulary list on the board for follow-up after the discussion session.)

The brainstorming session is goal oriented. Students know that they are preparing for a meeting with community representatives regarding health careers and community safety. Brainstorming is done first in pairs. Ask students to think of two or three questions they have about procuring health care services in this city. Encourage them to think of additional questions they would like to ask when they visit the local hospital.

After five minutes, ask students to end their discussion and call attention to the vocabulary list the teacher has put on the board during their discussion. Ask if there are any unfamiliar terms. Give any needed explanation if the class is unable to offer it. Such words might include: emergency room ambulance health insurance prenatal care postnatal care immunization AIDS.

Direct students to group in fours and share their list of questions. Each group of four will come up with a single list of questions. Move among the groups checking to keep students on task and to offer help if needed. Encourage students to check for any duplications. Allow 7–10 minutes for the group of four to come to agreement on which questions to select.

With the whole class, ask each group to submit their questions. Remind them that if the question has already been raised they need not repeat it. Direct four students (one from each group) to record all the questions so that copies can be made and distributed before the end of the session. These questions will be taken home so that students can decide if the questions should be asked during the hospital visit at the end of the week. If videotaping will be done during the question-and-answer period, tell students in advance and explain that the class will view the tape at a following class to see how well they did and think of ways to improve for the next field trip.

Explain that the students will be doing most of the talking during the visit to the hospital. The teacher will be there, but won't be in charge. 'We need to choose some class leaders for this trip.' Remind students that there will be three other field trips and that others will have a chance to lead when the time comes.

Ask for volunteers or choose two students who will coordinate the visit to the hospital. One student will introduce the class to the Community Relations Director and will call on those who ask questions during the session. The second student will watch the time and after 35 minutes end the questioning period and thank the hospital personnel on behalf of the class. The second student will also ask the hospital personnel if they have any questions for the students. The two student leaders meet with the teacher after class for any clarification. Remind students about the departure time for the field trip.

Activity: Day Two. Students will meet for a half-hour prior to leaving for the hospital. Review areas of responsibility. Ask for two volunteers to take notes to prepare a short report for the class newspaper. Find out if anyone has thought of additional questions to ask at the hospital. What about

The idea for this lesson is taken from 'Real reality revisited: An experimental communicative course in ESL' by Carol Montgomery and Miriam Eisenstein , *TESOL Quarterly* Vol. 19, June 1985. The lesson plan was designed by Gail Britanik.

employment opportunities at the hospital? Volunteer opportunities? Free community health examinations, etc. Encourage students to ask these questions at the appropriate time.

Students travel in the community van or cars to the hospitals and are met by the Community Relations Director. There is a brief meeting to welcome students, then a short tour of the facility is given. The group returns to the meeting room. The student leader introduces the class to the director and thanks her/him for welcoming the class. The director presents a 10-minute overview and invites students' questions. (This is according to an agreed-upon format between teacher and hospital personnel.) The instructor or an assistant videotapes the session. The second student leader, who is timing the session, intervenes to call time and to thank the director, inviting any questions from her/him. Students are reminded to write any thoughts about their visit in their notebooks before the next class session.

Post Activity: Day Three. Students are asked to gather in groups of three and to list five things they learned from the field trip. Then in the large group, the teacher asks if they found out the things they had hoped to learn? What things were unexpected? List these on the board. Ask students if they are ready to view the videotaped segment. Remind them that they will be watching and listening to see how well things went and to see how we might improve our questions when we visit the community bank or credit union. Following the video viewing, elicit feedback, asking students to list strengths and weaknesses. Record these on the chalkboard. Ask students who volunteered to write for the class newspaper to work on their two-paragraph reports. Ask for two student volunteers to write a note of thanks to the hospital personnel. The letter will be signed by the whole class during the next class session. Ask students to write in their notebooks: (1) 'The best things about our hospital trip were… '; and (2) 'I think we could improve by… '

Adaptation: If students are unable to visit a facility, community resource personnel can be invited to visit the class. Institutional brochures, video programmes, etc. can be used to supplement a guest speaker's presentation.

References

Bygate, M. (1988) Linguistic and strategic features of the language of learners in oral communication exercises. Unpublished PhD thesis. Institute of Education, University of London.
— (1988) Units of oral expression and language learning in small group interaction. *Applied Linguistics* 9, 59–82.

— (1992) Neither chaos nor magic: On the systematic influence of oral communication tasks on the language of learners. In *Working Papers*, Department of
Linguistics, University of Reading.

Cohen, E.G. (1986) *Designing Groupwork*. New York: Teachers College Press.

Danielson, D., Porter, P. and Hayden, R. (1990) *Using English, Your Second Language*
(second edition). Englewood Cliffs, NJ: Prentice-Hall.

— (1990) *Using English, Your Second Language: Instructor's Manual* (second edition).
Englewood Cliffs, NJ: Prentice-Hall.

Day, R. (ed.) (1986) *Talking to Learn: Conversation in Second Language Acquisition*.
Rowley, MA: Newbury House.

Dewey, J. (1910) *How We Think*. London: Heath & Co.

DiPietro, R. (1987) *Strategic Interaction*. New York: Cambridge University Press.

— (1990) Helping people do things with English. *English Teaching Forum* July, 35–38.

Doughty, C. and Pica, T. (1986) 'Information gap' tasks: Do they facilitate second
language acquisition? *TESOL Quarterly* 20 (2), 305–25.

Gaies, S.J. (1985) *Peer Involvement in Language Learning*. Englewood Cliffs, NJ:
Prentice-Hall.

Gass, S. and Marlos Varonis, E. (1985) Negotiation of meaning in non-native
speaker, non-native speaker conversation. In S. Gass and C. Madden (eds) *Input
and Second Language acquisition*. Rowley, MA: Newbury House.

Hendrickson, J.M. (1987) Error correction in foreign language teaching: Recent
theory, research, and practice. In M.H. Long and J.C. Richards (eds) *Methodology
in TESOL: A Book of Readings*. New York: Newbury House.

Klippel, F. (1984) *Keep Talking*. Cambridge: Cambridge University Press.

Krashen, S.D. (1980) The input hypothesis. In J.E. Alatis (ed.) *Georgetown University
Roundtable on Language and Linguistics* (pp. 168–80). Washington, DC: Georgetown University Press.

Long, M.H. (1977) Group work in the teaching and learning of English as a foreign
language: Problems and potential *English Language Teaching Journal* 31 (4),
285–92.

— (1985) Input and second language acquisition theory. In S. Gass and C. Madden
(eds) *Input and Second Language Acquisition* (pp. 207–25). Washington, DC:
Georgetown University Press.

— (1989) Task, group, and task-group interactions, *University of Hawai'i's Working
Papers in ESL* 8 (2), 1–26.

Long, M.H. and Crookes, G. (1992) Three approaches to task-based syllabus design.
TESOL Quarterly 26, 27–56.

Long, M.H. and Porter, P. (1985) Group work, interlanguage talk, and second
language acquisition. *TESOL Quarterly* 19 (2), 207–28.

McGroarty, M. (1989) The benefits of cooperative learning arrangements in second
language instruction. *NABE Journal* 13 (2), 127–43.

— (1991) What can peers provide? In J.E. Alatis (ed.) *Georgetown University
Roundtable on Language and Linguistics* (pp. 41–55). Washington, DC: Georgetown
University Press.

Neves, A. (1983) The effect of various input on the second language acquisition of
Mexican American children in nine elementary school classrooms. Doctoral
dissertation, Stanford University.

Nunan, D. (1989) *Designing Tasks for the Communicative Classroom*. Cambridge:
Cambridge University Press.

Pica, T. and Doughty, C. (1985). Input and interaction in the communicative language classroom: A comparison of teacher-fronted and group activities. In S. Gass and C. Madden (eds) *Input and Second Language Acquisition*. Rowley, MA: Newbury House.

— (1988) Variations in classroom interaction as a function of participation pattern and task. In Jonathan Fine (ed.) *Second Language Discourse* (pp. 41–55). Norwood, NJ: Ablex Publishing.

Pica, T., Young, R. and Doughty, C. (1987) The impact of interaction on comprehension. *TESOL Quarterly* 4 (21), 737–58.

Pica, T., Holliday, L., Lewis, N. and Morgenthaler, L. (1989) Comprehensible output as an outcome of linguistic demands on the learner. *Studies in Second Language Acquisition* 11, 63–90.

Porter, P. and Danielson, D. (1991) Handout from talk 'Addressing some criticisms of group work' at the Annual TESOL Convention, New York City.

Porter, P., Grant, M. and Draper, M. (1985) *Communicating effectively in English: Oral Communication for Non-native speakers* (second edition in press). Belmont, CA: Wadsworth.

Swain, M. (1985) Communicative competence: Some roles of comprehensible input and comprehensible output in its development. In S. Gass and C. Madden (eds) *Input and Second Language Acquisition*. Rowley, MA: Newbury House.

Tarvin, W.L. and Al-Arishi, A.Y. (1991) Rethinking communicative language teaching: Reflection and the EFL classroom. *TESOL Quarterly* 25 (1), 9–27.

Ur, P. (1981) *Discussions That Work: Task-centered Fluency Practice*. Cambridge: Cambridge University Press.

Yule, G., Powers, M. and MacDonald, D. (1992) The variable effects of some task-based learning procedures on L^2 communicative effectiveness. *Language Learning* 42 (2), 249–77.

9 One Peer Response Group in an ESL Writing Class: A Case Study

MARY CALDER

Because Zamel (1987) is concerned that research fails to inform pedagogy, she challenges ESL teachers to conduct their own research and to investigate the relationship between practice and writing development in the classroom. In response to Zamel's challenge, I undertook a study of one peer response group in a process-oriented writing class I taught at the University of Regina. The purpose of the study was to learn more about what actually happens in peer group conferences and how students help one another to improve in-progress writing drafts. To do this, a group of three intermediate level ESL students were audiotaped during two peer writing conferences. Transcripts were analysed and writing drafts written before and after conferences were compared to determine if and where revisions were made and to attempt to connect these changes to comments made during the conferences. The results of the study indicate that the group responses of the three participants serve to inform, direct, and elicit. As well, the writers appear to have developed three areas of writing skills: sense of audience, sense of voice, and sense of power in language.

Introduction

One classroom practice used extensively in my ESL writing classes is the peer response group. While I felt intuitively that this practice was successful for developing communicative competence, I wanted to learn more about what actually happens in peer groups. In order to investigate the relationship between this teaching practice and the writing development of my students, I conducted a naturalistic case study of one group in an intermediate ESL writing class I was teaching at the University of Regina.

Theoretical Framework

Based on the theoretical frameworks of communicative language teaching and collaborative learning, the instructional focus in process oriented writing classes is extended beyond the finished text to include text production and audience comprehension. According to DiPardo and Freedman (1987: 3), the following are key features of process instruction:

> It focuses on writing as a process, with instruction aimed at intervening in that process; it teaches strategies for invention and discovery; it emphasizes rhetorical principles of audience, purpose, and occasion, with evaluation based on how well a given piece meets its audiences needs; it treats the activities of pre-writing, writing and revision as intertwining, recursive processes; and it is holistic, involving nonrational intuitive faculties as well as reason.

Using peer groups in second language classes can be an effective practice to support the process paradigm. According to Long and Porter (1985), group work can increase the number of language practice opportunities, improve the quality of student talk, individualise instruction, create a positive affective environment, and increase student motivation. Groups provide opportunities for comprehensible input and interlanguage talk. By negotiating for meaning, students can offer each other genuine communicative practice. Mangelsdorf and Schlumberger (1992) suggest peer groups ensure students become actively involved in making meaning, not only receiving meaning.

Freedman (1992) concludes that peer groups are well suited to classrooms that de-emphasize the whole class, teacher dominated model. Group work provides the time and opportunity needed for thinking and talking about topics, as well as revising. Due to its interactive nature, collaboration increases student awareness that successful communication requires writers to develop a sense of audience because real people, classmates, read and respond to their work (Urzua, 1987). Groups provide an opportunity for writers to ask for help to solve problems and for readers to respond to the content. Writers benefit from response to their ideas and their writing throughout the writing process, not only when the final draft is evaluated (DiPardo & Freedman, 1987).

The Writing Class

In the Regina study, participants were attending two, two and a half hour writing classes for each of the semester's 12 weeks. Class activities included responding to readings, language study, journal writing and composition.

Students wrote in journals in class and outside of class to generate and explore ideas, as well as to develop automaticity, confidence, and speed (MacGowan-Gilhooly, 1991). They chose their own topics because when they do, they write quantitatively more and qualitatively better (Zamel, 1982); however, they were encouraged to select topics relevant to the course itself. For example, topics evolved during discussions of the text, *Amazing! Canadian Newspaper Stories*, or of video presentations, such as *Discuss It!*. Topics suggested in other discussions included the process of writing, the ESL programme and activities, and responses to other students' ideas. Discussion was intended to provide comprehensible input for writing.

Six journal entries were revised to become compositions written in an academic style and submitted for evaluation. During the composition activity, students read model paragraphs and learned what is expected in academic writing. Peer groups were organised so that three students could read and respond to each other's work in progress. Students made up their own groups; membership changed when final drafts were completed in order to provide writers with a wide audience of readers.

The conference procedure was based on the Bell model (1991). Writers provided each reader with a photocopy of the text. Prior to reading, writers identified a problem they had with their work and asked for help solving it. Writers read their work aloud, not only to make reading more comprehensible, but also to learn to recognise for themselves what kinds of revision may be needed. The group discussed solutions to the writer's problem and readers identified strengths and weaknesses of the piece. Feedback was provided in oral and written form.

As the instructor, I participated in groups only when asked to clarify a point or answer specific questions. This approach shifts responsibility for and control of writing and learning from the teacher to the student (Zamel, 1987).

Data sources, data collection procedures and analysis procedures

Students Nie, Paula, and Yuki, the participants, moved to Regina immediately prior to the semester to enrol in the ESL programme. Nie, a graduate engineer from China, was 29 years old; Paula, from Malaysia, and Yuki, from Japan, were both 19-year-old high school graduates. Although this was the sixth and final set of peer group conferences, it was the first time Nie, Paula and Yuki had worked together.

Data for analysis included: (a) audiotapes of two conferences; (b) transcripts of audiotapes; (c) student journals; (d) first, second, and final drafts of compositions; (e) photocopies used by readers; and (f) informal student interviews.

Transcripts of six texts discussed during two conferences were compared with findings of the 1985 Gere and Stevens study in which student texts and transcripts were analysed to determine the apparent function of responses. The 1985 study indicates group responses serve to inform, direct and elicit.

According to Gere and Stevens (1985), the effectiveness of writing group responses is demonstrated in changes made in subsequent drafts. To analyse the changes, I compared the first and second drafts, as well as the second and third drafts, of each participant's work. In addition, response group discussions were compared with subsequent revisions. Results were also compared to the findings of Urzua's 1987 study of four ESL Southeast Asian children who appear to have developed three areas of writing skills: sense of audience, sense of voice, and sense of power in language.

Results of the Study

Regina readers responded to the writing throughout both conferences. For example, when Nie said: 'I think maybe my conclusion is very short, but I can't find another,' Yuki suggested: 'Chinese tea is very good,' and Paula added: 'Nothing can compare to Chinese tea'. Gere and Stevens (1985: 97) define response as an answer or reply offered in reaction to a specific stimulus. Their 1985 study found oral language in writing groups to be responsive because it focuses on the text in such a way that both the text and reader reaction to the text are acknowledged. The study identifies three language functions: to inform, direct, and elicit. These functions are found in this study as well. One example of each illustrates the findings. Nie's topic sentence was: 'In China, many people like to drink tea and there are many interesting story about rule and tea.' Readers expressed concern about the discrepancy between the topic sentence and supporting detail. The following comments serve to inform about the formal properties of the text.

Paula: Why do the people like Chinese tea? Is it good for your health or what?
Yuki: Why do people like to drink tea?
Nie: Many people like to drink tea but it's not my main idea.
Paula: Your problem is your topic.
Nie: Maybe yes, I have a problem. Yes.

Although Nie referred to two kinds of tea, Dragon Well and Chief of Monkey, he told only one story. Paula and Yuki were adamant he write both stories because he referred to two types of tea. The following conversation directs the writing process because it suggests content changes.

Yuki: How about this Dragon Well tea?

Paula: You have two examples: Dragon Well and Chief of Monkey.

Yuki: I want to know about this story, Dragon Well.

Nie: Maybe next time.

Paula: No, no. Here you say two examples, but down here you just give one example. It is not balanced, an error.

Nie: Do you know I just give one example. If I give more examples, I think it is too long.

Paula: But I want to know the Dragon Well story.

Paula wrote about grandparents living with grandchildren. Nie drew attention to a problem; he wanted to know when her story took place, 'The present or the past?' Yuki, too, requested more detail; she wanted to know the number of adults who did not want to live with their own parents. Such questions and comments draw the writer's attention to ambiguities and discourse problems.

Yuki: I think some people?

Paula: Some, not all.

Nie: Just some people?

Yuki: You have to write some; some parents…

Nie: Yes, I just thought every. Some parents don't want their children living with their grandfather.

Conversations cited above indicate Nie, Paula and Yuki developed a collaborative relationship to assist one another with direct and specific comments and questions. They demonstrate the group's attempts to inform, direct and elicit, supporting the 1985 findings regarding language function in peer groups.

Following group discussion, writers expected to revise the subsequent draft. According to Urzua (1987), group responses that lead to and shape revision help ESL writers develop a sense of audience. For example, in response to questions about why dew on flowers makes the best tea, Nie answered: 'It is very good for your skin; if you drink tea made with dew, when you are 50 years old, you just look 20 years old.' Yuki suggested Nie add: 'That is good for health and that can make girl keep beautiful forever.' It appears Nie respected Yuki's advice enough to incorporate it. Urzua concludes the immediacy of feedback appears to dramatically influence writing development.

Urzua (1987) suggests deciding what to revise and what not to revise may develop an emerging sense of voice. Voice, according to Graves (cited in Urzua: 289), is the imprint of ourselves on our writing. Responding to a Malay newspaper article about a man refusing to let his parents live with his children, Paula stated defiantly: 'I can tell you my opinion. I hate this guy because I love my grandparents very much.'

Nie and Yuki advised Paula, 'Add your opinion.' When Paula did this, her sense of voice became more powerful. In the third draft, Paula further personalised the text by including her own experience of living with her grandmother. The additions made Paula's voice increasingly clear.

Nie, on the other hand, did not feel obliged to follow the reader's advice. Although discussion transcripts of Nie's two drafts are more than twice as long as the others, he made fewer revisions. In fact, following a lengthy discussion of the second draft, Nie merely recopied the second draft text for the third draft, making additional mechanical errors. This is significant for two reasons; both readers were adamant Nie add the Dragon Well story and Nie, himself, asked for help to improve the conclusion.

According to Urzua (1987), it is largely through revision, where language can be manipulated and rearranged, that students can better appreciate a sense of the power of language. In the second draft, Yuki wrote: 'We have to keep the good balance.' Nie did not understand what she was writing about so he suggested: 'You should explain balance'. In the second draft, Yuki wrote: 'We have to keep the number of the wild animals.' In the third draft, the idea was further refined: 'We have to protect the number of wild animals'.

Confused by the conclusion: 'We have to keep the number of wild animals and we have to keep the place where wild animals live', Nie asked Yuki, 'Do you mean people should give the chance or the place to let animals live?' When Yuki said: 'a place', Nie questioned: 'Such as a national park?' Yuki answered: 'It's a place to protect wild animals like a national park.' In the final draft, she added: 'We have to keep places where they live like Banff National Park.' Yuki adopted Nie's idea to support her argument. Discussion appears to have helped participants develop greater awareness of the power of language.

The three participants did revise subsequent drafts based on information, direction and questioning feedback from their peers. Changes reflect apparent advances in the understanding and use of writing processes as students interacted with the meaning and content of each text. For each writer, changes resulted in the production of a more effective and more meaningful piece (see Appendices). Writing appears to have become an act of communication about content important to writer and reader (Zamel, 1987). Comparison of in-progress drafts and final drafts reveals that the three Regina participants, like the four ESL students in Urzua's study, appear to have developed a sense of audience, a sense of voice and a sense of power in language.

Conclusion

Findings of this study indicate that in one peer response group in a process-oriented writing class, students collaborated to provide effective feedback for one another. Like the students in the Gere and Stevens (1985) study, Regina students also addressed questions of meaning and content, rather than editing concerns. Analysis of group discussion transcripts and subsequent revisions reveals that writers developed skills of self-direction and critical reflection to produce more fluent and proficient writing. In my opinion, Nie, Paula and Yuki wrote better pieces and with more confidence and enjoyment as a result of participating in a peer response group. Their comments to me suggest they developed a more positive attitude toward writing; writing became important for its own sake, not merely as an evaluation tool for passing the course.

Zamel (1982) suggests syntax, vocabulary, and rhetorical form, important features of writing, need to be taught not as ends in themselves but as the means to express a message. In this group, students did attend to semantics and syntax when revising. I believe one significant aspect of the process paradigm is the emphasis on students identifying and confronting their own problems. It appears that the ability to revise develops and improves when writers confront problems in their own work.

Instructional classroom practice is most effective when based on sound theoretical foundations. This study, developed from communicative language teaching and collaborative learning frameworks, finds the process approach to writing was successful for three ESL writers. By investigating the interactions of one peer response group in my own classroom, I have learned how the participants helped one another improve in-progress writing drafts and, as a result, write better compositions. I conclude that using the peer response group is a teaching practice that proved effective for developing the communicative competence of the three participants of this study.

Appendix 1

Nie's final draft: Tea in China

In China, many people like to drink tea and there are many interesting story and rule about tea.

There are many kinds of famous tea in China. The famous tea such as 'Dragon Well' and 'Chief of Monkey' have some nice folklores. For example, Why do people call the tea 'Chief of Monkey'? There is a story about the tea. Long ago, there is a kind of tea plant on the mountains which nobody can climb up. One day, a person found that some monkeies often picked leafs of the tea plant and offered the tea leafs to the chief of their groups. So the person tried to get some leafs of the tea plant and had a cup of the tea, he found that the tea tasted very nice. Then, many people began to plant a lot of the kind of tea plants and call the kind of tea 'Chief of Monkey'.

In China, here are many rule about drinking tea. The different kinds of tea should use different temperture water and different area's water. People think that you could get very nice different taste of tea according to the rule. It is said that the dew on flowers is the best water to drink tea, and the drinking is good for health, and can make girl keep beatuful for ever, but nobody has collected a cup of dew to drink tea.

I like to drink tea and the folklores about tea.

Appendix 2

Paula's final draft: Grandparents living with grandchildren

Some parents don't like their children to live with their grandparents. There is a real story in Malay newspaper. I am surprised by that. Children don't know why their parents act so, and they try to get answer from them. The answer is that their grandparents are old fashion people and they don't have good education background. Because of this reason, the parents are scared that their children will be influenced by their grandparents, their way of thinking, acting, etc. On the other hand, the grandparents are very angry about this. They love and care for the grandchildren. Although they don't have good education, they still can do their best to let their grandchildren know what is right and what is wrong. When they are growing up. Because in a way, knowledge is not the most important thing in the world. Even if they have knowledge, they don't use them in the people way, it's still useless. How to be a good person is more important. So they don't think it's fair to separate them with their grandchildren.

In my opinion, I feel it is unfair for the grandparents too. Because my grandparents lived with us. My grandfather passed away before I was born. But my grandmother loved me very much. She liked to tell us stories about herself, about the war, about something which can teach us what is right and what is wrong in our daily life. And I learn a lot from her. So I think those parents who don't allow their children to stay with their grandparents are wrong. Old people have more experience. They can teach their grandchildren a lot of good things. It will benefit the grandchildren in their future.

Appendix 3

Yuki's final draft: Wild animals

Many wild animals are killed by human beings. We have to stop killing them at random, and we have to protect them. Now some of wild animals are almost dying out and many of them are decreasing every year. For example, many African elephants are killed to get their ivory tusks, but killing elephants is illegal. Much ivory is smuggled into Japan, and there, the ivory is used to make impressions for family seals that are used for signatures. But they can be made from plastics. As well, many baby seals are killed in Canada to get their white fur, because human beings want their fur. When they grow up, their fur will change to a dark colour. We must not kill animals at random, and we must not destroy nature for our convenient life. We have to protect the number of the wild animals, and we have to keep places where they live like Banff National Park. It is a big problem to protect wild animals, but we should be able to solve it.

References

Bates, S. (1991) *Amazing! Canadian Newspaper Stories*. Scarborough, Ontario: Prentice-Hall Canada Inc.

Bell, J. (1991) Using peer response groups in ESL writing classes. *TESL Canada Journal* 8 (20), 65–71.

DiPardo, A. and Freedman, S. (1987) Historical overview: Groups in the writing classroom (Technical Report No. 4). Berkeley, CA: Center for the Study of Writing.

Freedman, S. (1992) Outside-in and inside-out: Peer response groups in two ninth-grade classes. *Research in the Teaching of English* 26 (1), 71–107.

Gere, A. and Stevens, R. (1985) The language of writing groups: How oral response shapes revision. In S. Freedman (ed.) *The Acquisition of Written Language: Response and Revision* (pp. 85–105). Norwood, NJ: Ablex.

Long, M. and Porter, P. (1985) Group work, interlanguage talk, and second language acquisition. *TESOL Quarterly* 19 (2), 207–228.

MacGowan-Gilhooly, A. (1991) Fluency before correctness: A whole language experiment in college ESL. *College ESL: A Journal of Theory and Practice in the Teaching of English as a Second Language* 1 (1), 37–47.

Mangelsdorf, K. and Schlumberger, A. (1992) ESL student response stances in a peer-review task. *Journal of Second Language Writing* 1 (3), 235–54.

National Film Board of Canada (1992) *Discuss It!* Montreal: Author.

Urzua, C. (1987) 'You stopped too soon': Second language children composing and revising. *TESOL Quarterly* 21 (2), 279–304.

Zamel, V. (1982) Writing: The process of discovering meaning. *TESOL Quarterly* 16 (2), 195–209.

— (1987) Recent research on writing pedagogy. *TESOL Quarterly* 21 (4), 697–715.

10 Correction of Speech Errors: Some Suggestions

PIERRE DEMERS and GUYLAINE BÉRUBÉ

This chapter proposes three practical techniques to correct speech errors of intermediate L2 learners: the gestural, peer, and echoing correction techniques. The use of these techniques can facilitate the development of strategies for self-correction, without interfering with the development of communication skills.

Introduction

The growing importance L2 teachers give to the communicative approach creates certain problems, one of the most important being how the correction of errors is made.

Because emphasis is put on the message, very little attention is sometimes given to the form and many teachers no longer correct the learners' errors (Bess & Porquier, 1988).

Different researchers in the field (Obadia 1987; Narcy 1992) have formulated strategies aimed at the correction of mistakes. Calvé, (1992: 458) writes: 'To correct or not to correct is not the question.' It is more important, he says, not to interfere with the message. Any correction of errors must respect this principle.

According to Calvé the four main correction techniques are (from the most to the least effective) self-correction, peer correction, indirect correction and systematic correction by the teacher.

The idea of self-correction is not new, since it goes back at least to Sapir (1970), and many teachers will have already used it either with the aid of a video or a traditional language laboratory. However, the challenge is to have the student self-correct (thus increasing his linguistic awareness) without interfering with the communication process. In other words, how is it possible to check upon the form when the goal of the course is to concentrate on the message?

The techniques presented in this chapter (gestural, peer and echoing) have as their objective an increase in the learner's self-correction abilities. The time required for students to develop this ability will vary depending on the particular components of the situation.

Gestural Correction

In order to practise this technique, the teacher has to stick to precise proxemics and help students recognise what errors they have made without interfering with the communication process.

Proxemics

Each student must be able to see all the other students as well as the teacher and be seen by all the other students. Therefore, the traditional circle (closed or open) disposition of the classroom can be maintained as long as the teacher is outside the circle, always moving and diagonally opposed to the student who speaks. This way, the teacher can address a maximum of students and be seen by the student whose speech is being corrected.

The role of the other students (the ones who are listening) is to focus their attention upon the message while the role of the teacher is to focus upon both the message and the form.

The gestures

The correcting gestures may vary from one teacher to another but it is important that the students be aware that these gestures are used to correct their errors. The following gestures work well in practice and are given as examples (see illustrations in the Appendix):

(1) A pointed finger towards the student indicates that an error has been made while the other hand indicates which type of error has been committed.
(2) The hand movement that usually indicates to a car driver to move back indicates to use the past tense.
(3) The hand movement that usually indicates to a car driver to move forward indicates to use the future tense.
(4) The hand gesture used to indicate to speed up is used to tell the student to increase speech delivery.
(5) By putting a hand to one's ear, one indicates to the student to speak louder.
(6) The swaying of the hand indicates to change the order of words.

(7) The flickering of a finger indicates to add a word (a conjunction or a preposition for example).

(8) A circular gesture from left to right tells the student to continue with the idea or to complete the sentence.

(9) A halting gesture of the index underlines the need to reformulate the idea or rephrase the sentence.

(10) Finally, a gesture that expresses satisfaction (for example, the one used by Italians to indicate that a dish is delicious) could underline the student's good performance, especially if a commonly produced error has been omitted.

The list of gestures proposed here is not exhaustive because each teacher should adapt the gestures to students' needs and his or her personality.

Peer Correction

The goal of this technique is to have the students aware of the mistakes of their peers and make their peers aware of their own particular mistakes.

In order to do this, the teacher first has to underscore the most common mistakes: this could imply a short lesson on the particular forms to be corrected. According to certain authors (Porquier & Frauenfelder, 1980), it is important for students to understand not only their errors but why they make them. For example, students learning an L2 make errors stemming from their mother tongue and it would be important for teachers to make students aware of this. This way, the student does not feel as uncomfortable when an error is repeated over and over again.

Then, when a student speaks, the other students should relate form to the message. For example, when a student makes a common mistake, another student could make him aware of that mistake by formulating a question with the same content in its proper form, thereby providing the student with more than one teacher.

Of course, when this method is used, only certain mistakes are corrected: the most important and frequent ones, the ones that interfere with communication.

The result of this procedure is that the students gradually develop a sense of grammaticality without being afraid to make mistakes. The teacher's role is therefore to create a friendly and enjoyable atmosphere in the classroom so that the students gradually feel comfortable correcting one another, this atmosphere being recognised by many specialists as the golden way to L2 acquisition (Krashen, 1981).

The Echoing Correction Technique

The teacher first presents a mini lesson on the forms to be corrected. Then, when the student makes one of the mistakes previously discussed, the teacher echoes the student's mistake (thus making the student aware of it). According to Hendrickson (1978:396), 'several language specialists propose that once students are made aware of their errors, they may learn more from correcting their own errors than by having their teachers correct them'. It is important to say that the teacher needs to echo exactly what the student has said, providing a cue for the student to correct the mistake but not giving the correct form right away. If the student does not respond to the cue, then the teacher should provide the student with the correct form.

This technique differs from classical echoing because it allows the student to correct his own mistake before providing the correct form and enough time for the student to develop a feeling of self-correction.

Conclusion

The three techniques presented in this chapter offer the learners different strategies to help them correct their mistakes. The main objective is to develop strategies for self-correction that will eventually be integrated by the learners, giving them the chance not only to correct their mistakes but also avoid them by using the proper forms in the first place.

For a very long time, L2 methods and techniques focused too much on form. Now, with the communicative approach, not enough emphasis is placed on error correction. As suggested by recent models of a multidimensional curriculum developed in Canada for the teaching of French as a second language (Flewelling, 1992, for example), L2 pedagogy of the 1990s should try to integrate different (communicative and grammatical) approaches.

Appendix

(The drawings are by Ms. Hélène Tremblay)

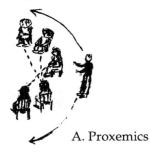

1.   A. Proxemics   B. Gestures

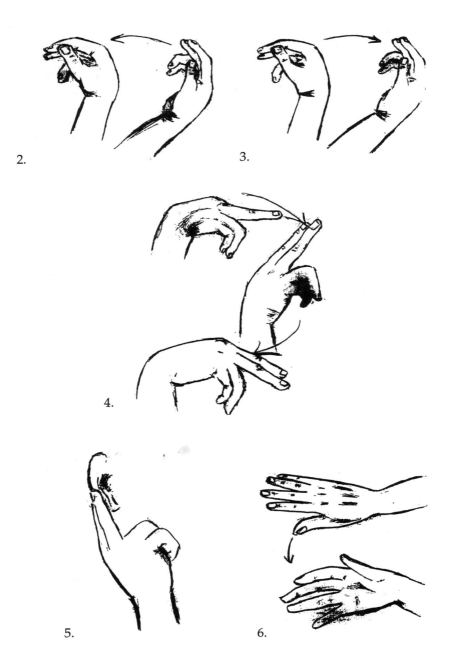

2.

3.

4.

5.

6.

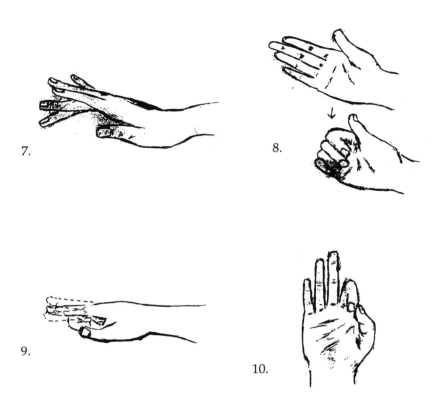

7.

8.

9.

10.

References

Bess, H. and Porquier R. (1988) *Grammaires et didactique des langues*. Paris: Hatier-Crédif.

Calvé, P. (1992) Corriger ou ne pas corriger, là n'est pas la question. *La revue canadienne des langues vivantes* 3 (48), 458–71.

Flewelling, J. (1992) Implications of the national core French study for FSL teachers. *Contact* 11 (3), 7–10.

Hendrickson, J. (1978) Error correction in foreign language teaching: Recent theory, research and practice. *The Modern Language Journal* 8, 387–98.

Krashen, S. (1981) *Second Language Acquisition and Second Language Learning*. Pergamon: Oxford.

Narcy, J. (1992) La prise de conscience des problèmes linguistiques conduit-elle à une réduction des erreurs commises en production libre. In *Acquisition et enseignement-apprentissage des langues* (pp. 345–54). Grenoble: LIDELEM:

Obadia, A. (1987) Procédés de prévention ou de correction des fautes orales en immersion. In P. Calvé et A. Mollica (eds) *Le français langue seconde: des principes à la pratique*. Welland: La revue canadienne des langues vivantes.

Porquier, R. and Frauenfelder U. (1980) Enseignants ou apprenants face à l'erreur: ou de l'autre côté du miroir. *Le Français dans le Monde* 154, 29–36.

Sapir, E. (1970) *Le langage*. Paris: Payot.

11 Collaborative Strategies for Narrative Structure

WILLIAM T. FAGAN

Students learning a second language are often lacking in effective strategies for reading, and writing. One such strategy identified by research is that of understanding, recalling and writing narrative structure. This chapter presents several activities for developing effective strategies of this nature. These strategies are developed through working from the known to the unknown, through capitalising on reader based knowledge and through collaborative effort.

Meeting the needs of second language learners is a multifaceted endeavour. The learners must have exposure to the target language and must also acquire strategy proficiency in completing various academic tasks. Information must be presented in a format that is comprehensible and the learners must have opportunity to collaborate with peers in various learning situations. This paper focuses on the role of strategy teaching in a collaborative setting in fostering second language learning.

Support for Collaborative Strategy Learning

Ineffective learning by students of a second language tends to result more from a lack of learning strategies rather than from such factors as inherent storage or capacity deficits (McLaughlin *et al.*, 1983). Huestis' (1991) research with 12- and 13-year-old ESL students also demonstrated the need for strategy teaching. While Duran (1987) contended that second language learners' comprehension may be explained in terms of the level of comprehension tasks (from vocabulary to literal meaning to inference, etc.) to which they were exposed and that there would be a progression of learning from the lowest level to the highest, Huestis' data did not confirm this. Rather, Huestis showed that the difficulty of a task was more dependent on whether it involved a greater use of background knowledge or text information, and particularly if the text information was influenced by strategy use. The ESL students in his study scored particularly low on the recognition of text structure/genre; they were more likely to try to recognise similarity of structure on the basis of cues such as the commonalty of vocabulary/content as opposed to organisational cues that reflected the text structure. Without a strategy for analysing text structure, the students' recognition of comparable structure reflected a superficial level of comprehension (Duran, 1987). Huestis recommended that specific strategies for recognising and understanding text structure be taught ESL students at this level.

Strategy learning, to be most effective, should be developed so that it supports and is supported by other aspects of learning. It has long been argued, for example, that reading and writing strategies should be developed conjointly since both are constructive processes with emphasis on meaning making (Fagan, 1992; Rubin & Hansen, 1984; Tierney & Pearson, 1983). Reading and writing are considered collaborative processes with many similarities. Rather than viewing reading as receptive and writing as expressive, these authors suggest viewing them as constructive processes. That is, the main objective of both is to construct meaning. Readers construct meaning from information presented in the text and from their own goals and prior knowledge frameworks. Readers are both receptive and expressive as part of this meaning construction process. By interjecting and interrelating their own goals and prior knowledge they are expressing new ideas while at the same time being recipients of this information which is being stored in memory for future use. In a similar manner, writers construct meaning by combining their goals and prior knowledge frameworks with language structures. They express their meaning via language and continually monitor or receive information as they compose which then influences the continued construction of meaning. When they have completed a piece of writing, they have expressed a goal and particular meaning, while at the same time being recipients of what they have constructed.

Furthermore, the use of oral language in collaborative settings should allow for greater learner participation and for providing a context in which learners are free to share their knowledge and construct meaning as they learn from each other (Buchanan, 1992). Rogoff (1990) argues for the importance of both peer and adult interaction. She maintains that adults play a supporting, directing and modelling role. Adults can guide the learners through various activities while modifying their language input so that the second language learners are more easily able to comprehend. Peer interaction while providing language input also provides emotional support. Rogoff (1990:183) reminds us that 'children spend far more time in direct interaction with one another than with adults'. The importance of emotional support is documented by Seliger (1988:30) who maintains that such support will often 'determine the role and degree of second language learning'.

Activity 1: Reading and Understanding Narrative Structure

Objectives

(i) Students will collaborate with peers and the teacher in learning.
(ii) Students and teacher will develop a set of rules for collaborative learning.
(iii) Students will generate appropriate background knowledge.
(iv) Students will read a story and then go through each step of a narrative plan.
(v) Students will be provided with a narrative plan for future use.

Comprehensible input

The focus is on modifying and supporting input so that it is comprehensible. The teacher should integrate oral and written language, such as writing a word on the board that is the focus of discussion, provide visual information such as diagrams and charts, and allow for peer interaction so that students with greater oral language proficiency can provide a model and support for others. There should be time for discussion and clarification to ensure a point is fully understood before moving on.

Step 1

Assign students to groups with not more that four or five to a group. Indicate that learning is more effective when learners have an opportunity to share knowledge, to question each other, clarify information and prepare questions for the teacher. Provide a few brief rules for collaborating:

(a) Choose a leader who will raise questions/points with the teacher. (The leader should change with each new activity so that all get an opportunity to take this role.)
(b) The leader should describe/explain the assigned task and ensure that all members of the group understand their goal.
(c) Each member of the group should get a chance to participate in the discussion.
(d) The leader should ask if anyone has questions or is not clear about something.
(e) The leader should summarise the results of the discussion and ask if there are any additions/clarification.

Step 2

Introduce the activity by developing an analogy to which the learners can relate narrative structure. Set the following questions for each group:

(a) Think of all the parts of this school building (classrooms, offices, etc.). List as many as you can.
(b) Why is it easy for you to find your way around the school building now?
(c) Why was it difficult to find your way around on your first visit to the school?

Allow each group leader to share the results of the discussion. If possible, have a plan (rough sketch) of the school building and summarise the discussion by indicating that all the students now have a 'plan of the school in their heads' which they can use to better understand and find their way around the school building.

Print the word 'narrative' on the board and emphasise the pronunciation. Point out that in today's lesson the class will be studying narrative text and that they will develop a plan for narrative text which will help them understand and use narrative.

Step 3

Assign a short story such as that given below.

A Trip to the Bank

Tom Ford was awake early. The sun was shining brightly and he could hear the birds singing. It was still four hours before the bank opened. He had seen the truck of his dreams and he wanted to get the money for a downpayment as soon as possible. His old truck had just quit and he needed a truck in order to do his work as a handyman.

Tom was too restless to do anything else so he took the bus downtown. He had breakfast at a small diner and then walked over towards the bank. It was still an hour before opening time.

Suddenly, Tom noticed there was something going on at the bank. A man ran out the door. Tom could see a gun in his hand and he quickly hid behind a parked car. Then another man ran from the bank. They got into a van and sped off.

Tom rushed to the bank. The manager and staff were tied up but they were not hurt. He untied them and they called the police. Tom was able to remember the licence number of the van. He had to wait awhile but finally he was able to get his money. He rushed out of the bank to catch the bus for the used car and truck lot.

Print the title on the board and draw on the students' background knowledge to develop an appropriate schema. Tell the students that Tom (write the name on the board) is the main character/person of the story and when he went to withdraw money from his account at the bank, many unexpected things happened.

Have each group read the story as a group – sharing information such as word recognition, when necessary. Then read the story together with the whole class.

Step 4

Begin to develop a plan for the narrative by drawing a line from the word 'Narrative' and printing 'Characters'.

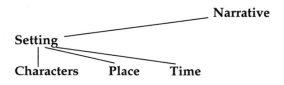

Narrative

Characters

Ask if there were other characters besides Tom. Ask where the action took *place* and the *time* when it occurred. Add these to the diagram and provide the heading, 'Setting', indicating that characters, place, and time provide the setting in a narrative.

Narrative

Setting

Characters   **Place**   **Time**

In a similar manner, talk about the action of the narrative in terms of goal, actions, reactions/feelings and outcome. As each is discussed, include the label in the diagram until the result looks like:

Narrative   **Event**
Setting

Characters Place Time   **Goal Actions Reactions Outcome**

Step 5

Have each group now reread the narrative and match information to the parts of the diagram. As the leaders share the information, slot it into a diagram on the board and enlist other groups to add omitted information.

Step 6

Give the learners a copy of a narrative structure (Appendix – Form 1). Have them realise that the same information from the diagram in step 4 is included here. Have them pretend that they are entering a narrative (building analogy) at the Title and let them think through the parts of a narrative that they would expect to find in each segment of the diagram.

Note: The students will need practice with several narratives before moving to the next activity.

Activity 2: Recalling Narrative Structure

Objectives

(i) Students complete a narrative plan after a brief story.

(ii) Students recall a story and tape it for analysis.

(iii) Students improvise on a story with the help of a narrative frame.

Comprehensible input

As indicated for Activity 1.

Step 1

Give each learner a narrative plan as a worksheet.

Step 2

Tell a brief story. After you finish, have the learners work as a group to slot information into the different parts of the plan.

Step 3

Have your own plan prepared beforehand, if possible, on an overhead. Show this and ask the groups how (if) their plans differ.

Step 4

Allow the learners to work in groups and assign them a story to read.

Step 5

Ask one group (different students might contribute different parts) to recall the story and tape record it.

Step 6

Play back the tape and ask the other groups to help slot this information into the appropriate place in the narrative plan.

Step 7

Provide the groups with a story and a partially completed plan (for example, you may write in the place, the goal, and one of the actions). Ask the groups to read the story and complete the plan.

Step 8

At a greater level of independence, ask the learners to read a story and then, without referring to the story, to write as much as they can remember. Have them slot this information on a narrative plan worksheet and indicate any omissions in their recall. This activity can also be grouped with monitoring performance, as the learners may initially be asked to rate their written recall on a scale of 1–10. After they match their recall with the narrative plan, they may be asked to rate it again.

Activity 3: Writing Narrative Structure

Objectives

(i) Students complete a narrative frame based on a story they have just read.

(ii) Students analyse a poorly written story and improve it.

(iii) Students write their own stories with teacher support.

(iv) Students share their stories with their peers.

(v) Peers develop modes of responding that are consistent with emphasis on narrative structure.

Comprehensible input

As indicated in Activity 1.

Step 1

Introduce writing narrative by using a narrative frame (Armbruster, 1990) for a story that has been read. Ask the students to complete it either singly or in groups. A narrative frame based on the story (*A Trip to the Bank*) is as follows:

This story is about _____ who wished to _____.
He felt _____ when he noticed _____.
Then he _____
_____.
Finally, he was able to _____.

Step 2

Discuss the notion of reader as editor. To develop this concept, hand out copies of a newspaper and talk about the role of reporters/writers and of the editor.

Step 3

Provide a story that is poorly written. In groups, have the students analyse it according to their narrative plan and note parts that could be improved (for example, the goal may not be clear).

Step 4

Have each group rewrite the story and then share their rewriting with the class.

Step 5

Ask students to write their own stories and conference with them as they do so.

Step 6

Ask them to look at their plan while thinking through a story that they want to write. As you move around the class, always direct your questions/comments so that it is clear as to which part of the plan they relate. For example, you might say, 'I'm curious about how your aunt *felt* when she discovered that she had picked up the wrong purse', 'I like the way you have developed information about your *character*, Elisa', 'I'm interested in more *action*. Tell me more about what happened between the time Tran took the train in Montreal and arrived in Winnipeg.'

Step 7

Help the learners develop the skill of asking questions/making comments about parts of a narrative. Read a short narrative to the class. After a particular segment has been read, have the students name the part of the story (according to the plan) and raise any questions or comments.

Step 8

Have students read to the class, stories they have written. The remainder of the class are asked to share in the reading by raising a question/comment about a particular part of the story. For example, a student might say, 'I have a question about the *setting*. What time of day did Karl receive the phone call?'

Note: Each of the above activities is best developed initially with short, single-event narratives. Eventually, the learners may move to longer narratives. This can be easily done through reading longer narratives, and through writing by expanding a narrative that has been written. For example, the narrative, *A Trip to the Bank*, could be expanded by having the learners continue the story with two more events:

(a) Tom arrives at the car and truck lot to discover that he is missing some money.
(b) Tom gets a reward.

Conclusion

Triangulation means to approach a task from a number of perspectives (at least three) which allows for more effective learning (Tompkins & Hoskisson, 1991). The activities described in this chapter highlight the concept of triangulation. Learning a second language is not only supported by oral language input, but by visual aids, strategy emphasis, and collaborative support. The students are active participants rather than passive recipients in these activities.

Comprehension, according to Pearson and Johnson (1978:24) consists of 'building bridges between the new and the known'. Pearson (1984) points out that as readers make meaning they tend to range between text-based processing and reader-based processing. The activities described above allow readers to build bridges between what they know (using plans) and the unknown (application of plans to understanding narrative structure). The students are able to draw on familiar surroundings for which they are more likely to have oral language labelling proficiency and use this information in understanding a more abstract concept.

The activities include text-based processing in which the focus is on intra-text structure, and reader-based processing which entails contributing, constructing, and sharing knowledge based on prior knowledge and using oral language proficiency. Both the comprehensive and comprehensible nature of the activities should enhance second language learning.

References

Armbruster, B. (March, 1990) Learning from reading: Using graphic organisers. Paper presented at the Washington Organization Reading Development Conference, Tacoma.

Buchanan, R. (1992) Dr. Marion Crowhurst's workshop on promoting active learning. *Teaching and Learning Newsletter* (Memorial University of Newfoundland) 8, 1–5.

Duran, R. (1987) Metacognition in second language. In J. Langer (ed.) *Language, Literacy and Culture: Issues of Society and Schooling* (pp. 49–63). Norwood, NJ: Ablex.

Fagan, W.T. (1992) *A Framework for Literacy Development: Effective Program and Instructional Strategies for Reading and Writing for Low-Achieving Adults and Children*. Montreal: Les Editions de la Chenelière.

Huestis, D. (1991) Levels of comprehension and meta-monitoring of 12 and 13 year old ESL and native English speaking readers. Unpublished doctoral dissertation. Edmonton, AB: The University of Alberta.

McLaughlin, B., Rossman, T. and McLeod, B. (1983) Second language learning: An information processing perspective. *Language Learning* 33, 135–58.

Pearson, P.D. (1984) A context for instructional research on reading comprehension. In J. Flood (ed.) *Promoting reading comprehension* (pp. 1–15). Newark, DL: International Reading Association.

Pearson, P.D. and Johnson, D.D. (1978) *Teaching Reading Comprehension*. New York: Holt, Rinehart & Winston.

Rogoff, B. (1990) *Apprenticeship in Thinking: Cognitive Development in Social Context*. Oxford: Oxford University Press.

Rubin, A. and Hansen, J. (1984) *Reading and Writing: How Are the First Two R's Related?* (Reading Education Report 5). Champaign, IL: University of Illinois, Center for the Study of Reading.

Seliger, H. (1988) Psycholinguistic issues in second language acquisition. In L.M. Beebe (ed.) *Issues in Second Language Acquisition*. Rowley, MA: Newbury House Publishing.

Tierney, R.J. and Pearson, P.D. (1983) Toward a composing model of reading. *Reading Education Report* 43. Champaign, IL: University of Illinois at Urbana-Champaign.

Tompkins, G.E. and Hoskisson, K. (1991) *Language Arts: Content and Teaching Strategies*. Toronto: Collier-Macmillan Canada, Inc.

Appendix Form 1: Narrative Structure

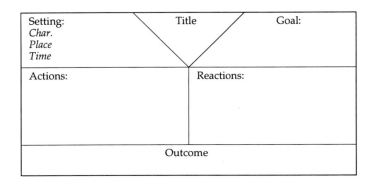

12 Writing a Short Story Through Sharing and Reflecting

MICHELLE CLÉMENT and DIANE LATAILLE-DÉMORÉ

In the context of a presentation to a target second language class, students are asked to produce an anthology which includes short stories. In so doing, they often experience difficulty identifying the different elements which constitute the narrative outline of a short story. Through sharing, and by reading and writing, students become aware of these elements, come to recognise them and eventually use them in their own writing.

Introduction

The activity described in this chapter is part of a process inspired by the multidimensional approach to second language teaching expounded by Stern (1983) and given concrete expression in the 'National Core French Study' (1990). The approach consists of starting with a communication situation which is meaningful to the student, and communicating this information at an appropriate language level that is also accurate in content. The student will achieve mastery of the task through an analysis of relevant source materials, task-based reflection, and a gradual progression from guided practice to autonomous writing.

According to Stern, this approach contains the following components: *language* (in this case, the short story); *communication* and *experience* as well as *culture* (the development of an anthology in the context of a presentation to a target language class); and *general language education* (knowledge transfer of the short story from one's first language to the target language and knowledge of short stories written by various authors in the student's first and second or foreign language).

More precisely, the activity described here stems from the *language* component, which aims at making learning more explicit (thus fostering retention), and providing the opportunities for the application of such knowledge. While purposely structured at the outset, these opportunities become more and more open and gradually lead to more spontaneous use.

The oral presentations and questioning which ensue foster 'objectiva-tion', that is, an analysis of the form of communication under study and a reflection of one's own performance (Painchaud, 1991:85–86). This meth-odology meets at least one of the conditions which facilitate the learning of the writing process in one's first language, as identified by Graves (Graves, 1983).

Finally, team work provides an opportunity for negotiation among peers and in itself constitutes a communication situation (Prabhu, 1987) and a learning experience with peers (Graves, 1983).

The activity described here aims at achieving the following objectives: As part of a team and given a specific context:

(1) The student shall identify the elements which constitute the narrative outline of a short story.
(2) The student shall prepare the outline of a short story which incorpo-rates these elements.
(3) The student shall present the outline to the class and improve it in accordance with the feedback given by his/her peers.

An Overview of the Process

In their second language class, students have been involved for some time in sharing their writing with a first language class. After being exposed to the elements of a narrative outline of a short story and the interpretation of various texts (Step 1), students are expected to draw up the outline of a short story and then share and analyse it with the whole class (Hardy *et al.*, 1990). Only later will they be asked to create a short story on their own (Step 3). The present report deals only with Step 2 (See Table 12.1).

Table 12.1 Overview of the process leading to the production of a short story

Step 1	Step 2	Step 3
Interpretation of several short stories. Identification of the structural elements of a short story.	Application of structural elements to the drawing up of an outline for a short story from a given context.	Production of a short story incorporating the structural elements of the short story.

The Process Within Step 2

(1) Preparation of an outline

(a) The class is divided into teams. Students may be allowed to form their own groups or this may be done at the teacher's discretion. Students' abilities are of utmost importance in the structuring of these teams in order to achieve a sense of balance and effective interaction among them (Johnson & Johnson, 1989).

(b) Each team is presented with a specific context and starting point. For example, 'It was a beautiful winter day. Everything seemed peaceful. They had come here on a holiday.'

This is an important step considering that the overall purpose is to help students acquire certain basic notions rather than create a story.

(c) Within a specific time established by the teacher, each team prepares an outline of a short story. The purpose is to identify the broader aspects and main elements which will constitute its framework. The following may be some of these elements:

- initial situation (time, setting, main character, action);
- disruptive event;
- incidents;
- climax;
- values (moral and social);
- final outcome.
  (See examples in Table 12.2.)

(d) After completing this task, each team decides the manner in which it will present its outline.

(2) Oral presentations

(a) Oral presentations may be made in random order or on a volunteer basis.

(b) Each team, in turn, delegates one or more spokespersons to present the main ideas of the story outlined earlier. While this occurs, the class attempts to identify, in writing, the elements of the proposed narrative outline. Students note as well the characteristics or aspects which may lead to questions, require explanations or simply appear to be interesting. A grid is designed for this purpose (See Table 12.3.).

Table 12.2 Example of an outline of a short story

(a) **Author:** a level 5 student
     Context:
     'It was a beautiful winter day. Everything seemed peaceful. They
     had come here on a holiday.'

(b) **Outline:**
     Initial situation
       Time: a holiday, winter, daytime, beautiful weather
       Setting: a cottage, near a lake, in the wilderness,
       Main characters: Mr Lachance, his sons Joël and Benoît, a friend,
       Action: an ice-fishing trip.

     Disruptive event
     Mr Lachance, Joël and Benoît set their fishing lines to try their luck.
     Everything seems peaceful, perhaps too much so.

     Incidents
       Once everything is set, Mr Lachance returns to the cottage for a
       rest while his two sons decide to go for a ride on their skidoo.
       Time goes by.
       Mr Lachance, now well rested, returns to check the lines. They
       are lying on the ice without bait. What has happened?
       Joël and Benoît return from their skidoo ride. Mr Lachance,
       obviously upset, starts questioning them.
       Lines are set again and everyone heads for the cottage to warm
       up.
       Time goes by.
       Everyone returns to check the lines and once again finds them
       undone. What has happened?
       This incident is repeated several times.
       While Mr Lachance is still suspicious about the boys, a plan is
       laid to find who is guilty.
       A little later, an animal is spotted close to the lines. It is likely the
       culprit! (CLIMAX)

     Final Outcome
       It is an otter, a clever animal, if any.
       Mr Lachance, Joël and Benoît decide to stay close to their lines
       from now on.

Table 12.3 Listening grid

1. **Initial situation**	1. **Initial situation**
(a) time	(a) _____
(b) setting	(b) _____
(c) main character(s)	(c) _____
(d) action	(d) _____
2. **Disruptive event**	2. **Disruptive event**
	_____
	_____
3. **Development**	3. Development
(a) two or three main incidents	(a) _____
	_____
(b) climax	(b) _____
4. **Final outcome**	4. **Final outcome**
	_____
	_____
5. **Description of main character**	5. **Description of main character**
(a) physical traits (2):	(a) _____
	_____
(b) psychological traits (2):	(b) _____
	_____
6. **Values**	6. **Values**
(a) moral or social	(a) _____
(b) example:	(b) _____
7. **Improvements to be made**	7. **Improvements to be made**
(a) suggestions	(a) _____
	_____

(c) Once the team has made its presentation, it questions the class on its structured outline (Table 12.4). It is the responsibility of the presenting team to assess the accuracy of the answers given and to make corrections if necessary. Thus, each team fosters the participation of all students in the analysis of the outline structure presented and helps the class integrate the basic notions presented earlier.

Table 12.4 Possible questions to be asked to the class by the presenting team

Examples:

Identify the initial situation as presented in our text?

What are: the disruptive events;
the climax;
the final outcome?

Has the narrator of the story: taken part in the action (participant);
seen it happen (witness);
or not (absent)?

Identify and describe the main character.

(d) The class now questions the presenting team about the various elements or aspects of the outline it presented. For example, students may wish to ask questions about the story's main character, setting, moral or social values, etc. The class is then invited to make suggestions on how to improve the structure of the short story. This must be done in a constructive way. Criticism must be avoided and group learning facilitated. The teacher ensures this through good classroom management, intervening only at moments deemed appropriate to make the necessary corrections, recommendations, or explanations.

(3) 'Objectifying' the activity

Once the oral presentations have been made, students return to their respective team to assess, in an interactive way, the outline of their short story. They are invited to modify and improve their joint production, where necessary. The sample grid devised for this purpose (Table 12.5) may be adapted to suit the teacher's needs.

Table 12.5 'Objectivation' grid

The outline of a short story	Yes	More or less	No
1. The initial situation is specified:			
(a) The main character's physical and/or psychological traits are revealed.			
(b) The setting is well described.			
(c) The time element (year, month, daytime or night, season, etc.) is identified.			
(d) A hint of the action to come is given.			
2. The disruptive event is introduced.			
3. A credible situation has been established.			
4. In the development:			
(a) The chronology of events has been respected.			
(b) The various incidents lead to the climax and final outcome.			
(c) The main character is revealed through his/her actions and reactions.			
5. The unexpected final outcome.			
6. The story captures our interest.			
7. *Overall impression*: On the reverse of this page, please note your comments regarding this group activity and state whether you are *very satisfied, satisfied,* or *more or less satisfied* with the result of your outline.			

Source: Adapted from Pierre Hardy *et al.*, *Unité d'apprentissage pour l'enseignement du français*, Cochrane-Iroquois Falls, Black River-Matheson.

Conclusion

Throughout this process, students have the opportunity of deepening their notions regarding the structure of a short story and perfecting their language skills. This step lies between the explanation and observation of the elements of a short story (Step 1) and their writing of that short story (Step 3). Students are provided with the opportunity to reflect on the structural elements of the short story as well as on the production of their own outline. By using this approach (based on a communication situation), students produce quality work which they are proud to share.

Glossary

(a) Class: Group of students of a given level.

(b) Context: A theme, idea, topic, sentence or beginning of a paragraph which serves as a starting point.

(c) Narrative outline: The structure of a literary text which includes the following elements: initial situation, disruptive event, incidents, climax and final outcome.

(d) 'Objectivation':   The process by which one returns to analyse and evaluate an accomplished task for the purpose of improving it. (Ontario Ministry of Education, 1987)

(e) Short story: A prose story with a full plot, generally brief, dramatic, and presenting a limited number of characters in situations which are plausible. It contains the following elements: setting, characters, values and narrative outline.

References

Graves, D.H. (1983) *Writing: Teachers and Children at Work*. Portsmouth: Heinemann.

Hardy, P., Levesque, M. and Chartrand, G. (1990) *Unité d'apprentissage pour l'enseignement du français, cycles intermédiaire, supérieur et CPO*. Conseil des écoles séparées du district de Cochrane-Iroquois Falls, Black River-Matheson.

Harley, B., D'Anglejan, A. and Shapson, S. (1990) *National Core French Study – The Evaluation Syllabus*. Ottawa: Canadian Association of Second Language Teachers (CASLT).

Hébert, Y. (1990). *Étude nationale sur les programmes de français de base – le syllabus formation langagière générale*. Ottawa: Association canadienne des professeurs de langues secondes.

Johnson, D.W. and Johnson, R. (1989) *Cooperation and Competition: Theory and Research*. Edina, MN: Interaction Book Company.

LeBlanc, C., Courtel, C., Trescases, P. (1990) *Étude nationale sur les programmes de français de base – le syllabus culture*. Ottawa: Association canadienne des professeurs de langues secondes.

LeBlanc, Raymond (1990) *National Core French Study – A Synthesis*. Ottawa: Canadian Association of Second Language Teachers (CASLT).

Ministère de l'Éducation et de la Formation de l'Ontario. (1987) *Programme-cadre de français: cycles intermédiaire et supérieur et cours préuniversitaire de l'Ontario*. Toronto: Auteur.

Painchaud, G. (1990) *Étude nationale sur les programmes de français de base – le syllabus langue*. Ottawa: Association canadienne des professeurs de langues secondes.

Robert, P. (ed.) (1985) *Petit Robert 1*. Montréal: Éditions Robert-Canada.

Prabhu, N.S. (1987) *Second Language Pedagogy*. Oxford: Oxford University Press.

Stern, H.H. (1983). *Toward a multidimensional foreign language curriculum*. In R.G. Mead (ed.) *Foreign Languages: Key Links in the Chain of Learning*. Middlebury, VT: Northeast Conference.

Tremblay, R., Duplantie, M. and Huot-Tremblay, D. (1990) *National Core French Study – The Communicative/Experiential Syllabus*. Ottawa: Canadian Association of Second Language Teachers (CASLT).

Evaluation: Oral Communication Assessment and the Portfolio Concept

JOSEPH E. DICKS and SALLY REHORICK

Portfolio assessment can be used to evaluate the oral communicative abilities of students in a formative way. By using a variety of evaluative techniques based on thematic units of a second language curriculum, a teacher can assess the ongoing development of her/his students and provide them with valuable diagnostic and global feedback. The theoretical construct, objectives, development, format and use of this kind of evaluation instrument are described.

Evaluation as Positive Experience: Portfolio Assessment

Portfolio assessment has become a very widely used and useful tool in many subject areas (Belanoff & Dickson, 1991). English language arts teachers, for example, have been employing portfolio assessment for many years. In portfolio assessment, teachers and students select from among different evaluation procedures at different times to provide a valid and representative picture of a given student's performance. Research in the area of evaluation clearly shows that certain students may perform poorly on a specific task (this tends to be particularly true for weaker students), while others may find the same task very easy. It is especially important that weaker students not be unfairly penalised because of their difficulty with a specific task which may result in a lower than normal representation of their performance. On the other hand, a portfolio is also meant to show progress and if only the best results are chosen, when initially the student may have experienced some difficulty, this would result in an inaccurate picture of the student's overall performance. The key to developing a meaningful portfolio is to choose those evaluations which provide a broad, representative sample of performance over a period of time.

Portfolio assessment, by its very nature, is performance-based evaluation: that is, an assessment of what students can *do* as opposed to what they *know*. The assumption underlying performance-based assessment is that by observing how well students perform specific tasks, one is able to estimate how well they will perform in real-life situations. Portfolio assessment is flexible and adaptable to specific situations. A valid assessment process must evaluate language performance in a variety of contexts which 'engages children in a wide range of language uses' (Antonacci, 1993:118). Due to restrictions of time and other unpredictable factors that enter into the day-to-day reality of the classroom, it may be that all different types of tasks will not be administered to all students in the process of evaluating a specific thematic unit. However, in the course of evaluating a number of different themes throughout a school year, it is possible to ensure that a given student would be evaluated using each type of technique several times.

Portfolio assessment provides an opportunity for learners to reflect in a meaningful way upon their language development. This reflection has important implications for students to become effective language learners, an ability which is receiving increasing attention in language syllabus design (LeBlanc, 1990). The process of consultation between teacher and students with respect to which techniques best reflect not only the students' performance at a specific point, but also which allow one to see the progress which has occurred over time, is extremely helpful in this respect.

A Case in Point: MOCAP

MOCAP is an acronym for a thematically based evaluation package entitled Maritime Oral Communication Assessment Portfolio. This is an evaluation package for French as a second language (FSL) which involves an evaluation of students' oral abilities, particularly as these are reflected in evaluative tasks which focus upon the communication of messages, ideas, opinions and feelings. Although MOCAP was developed for French as a second language, the principles and format of the evaluation techniques can apply to any second/foreign language. This evaluation package is intended to examine students' performance over an extended period of time so as to produce a portfolio containing a record of each student's progress on a variety of tasks over the course of a given unit of study, as well as a diagnostic assessment of students' major strengths and weaknesses.

MOCAP is composed of four evaluation modules, each representing grade level and programme approach. Core French is the basic program in which students study the language for approximately 30 – 45 minutes every day. French immersion is a programme in which students spend at least 50% of their time learning the second language through content subjects such as science, mathematics and social studies. Each of these modules contains a series of evaluation techniques that correspond to a specific theme. Each module represents a prototype and similar modules will be developed for use with other themes. As teachers become familiar with the various techniques, they will be in a position to develop their own variations according to the themes treated in class. In MOCAP, simulation techniques such as role-plays and surveys have been developed to represent key aspects of authentic communication within the context of a specific theme. It is this sort of evaluation which best reflects the principles of communicative competence and the thrust of the National Core French Study (LeBlanc, 1990).

In keeping with the *General Language Syllabus* (LeBlanc, 1990), MOCAP contains a self-assessment questionnaire which guides students in the process of reflecting upon their own performance and assessing their own strengths and weaknesses after participating in an evaluating activity. This questionnaire (see Appendix B), which would require some practice and guidance in the initial stages, could eventually provide extremely valuable feedback to students and teachers and could have a profound impact on students' own abilities to reflect on language use in a meaningful way. Teachers adapt this questionnaire as they see appropriate for use in their specific classroom situations.

Assessment Validity in a Communicative Context

MOCAP involves an evaluation of oral language performance. While the evaluation of reading and writing is also extremely important in a communicative approach, it is clear that the primary emphasis,in a great many second language programmes, is placed upon the development of functional communicative ability in oral language. MOCAP is designed for use at Grade 6 and Grade 9 in both core French and French immersion programmes. There are in effect four versions of MOCAP – one for each grade level and programme. However, it is recognised that the abilities of students vary from one situation to another and from year to year. If teachers at a given level find that, in general, the suggested tasks are either too easy or too difficult for their students, they are encouraged to explore tasks designed for another level and to experiment with these in their own classes. Similarly, if within a given class there are subgroups of students who may find tasks from another level more suited to their abilities, teachers could borrow from another level.

The main organising principle for MOCAP is thematic content. The various evaluation techniques developed for each level relate to a specific theme which was identified as being interesting and appropriate for students at that level. The evaluation is meant to be carried out in the context of a larger thematic unit of study, not in isolation. This thematic approach to evaluation was adopted to correspond with the recommendations of *The Communicative/ Experiential Syllabus* (Tremblay *et al.*, 1990) of the *National Core French Study* which maintains that *fields of experience* should be the organising principle of language learning. The themes treated in this assessment package (*leisure, food, travel* and *environment*) are related to a number of the fields of experience identified in the communicative/experiential (C/E) syllabus as being worthy of study for both their interest to students and their educational value. The *fields of experience* which have been treated in MOCAP and which are found in the C/E syllabus (Tremblay *et al.*, 1990:29–33) include: food-related experiences, physical activity type experiences, clothing related experiences, school related experiences, experiences with friends, experiences with conservation, experiences with consumerism, experiences with outdoor living, experiences with travel, and experiences with miscellaneous activities.

Evaluation of oral performance is in many ways the most difficult to conduct. With respect to the distinction between aural comprehension (listening) and oral production (speaking), MOCAP evaluates both elements simultaneously through a series of interactive situations. Indeed, MOCAP recognises that aural comprehension is a critical element in the process of interaction and negotiation (see for example Tremblay *et al.*, 1990). However, this is not to say that aural comprehension should not be evaluated as a separate activity in other contexts (on the contrary, at lower levels, in particular, students' listening abilities will be superior to their speaking ability and this should be recognised and reinforced).

In the case of oral evaluation of French second language abilities there are at least three major questions that must be answered before we can determine what kind of evaluation format we will use. First of all, we must know what will be the content of our test – what knowledge and skills do we expect students to possess in order to communicate? Secondly, we must know what we mean by the word communicate – what is the theory or construct of communication to which we ascribe? Thirdly, since we are talking about oral communication, we must know what we mean specifically by that term – what are the components of successful oral communication? Clearly, while these questions may be considered separately they address in effect three interrelated issues.

In answering the first question (skills and knowledge), we define the content of our evaluation instrument. If that content reflects the objectives of curriculum guides written for that level, and if classroom teachers can say that this content and these objectives reflect what is taught in their classes, then we can say that our test possesses *content validity*. This content and these objectives rarely exist in a vacuum. Usually they reflect a particular philosophy or approach to language teaching. This leads us to the second question (theory or construct). Since our evaluation instrument addresses communication in French as a second language, it should reflect the particular theory of communication that is found in the school systems in which this instrument will be used. In effect, this evaluation package has been elaborated according to the theoretical model of communicative competence proposed by Canale and Swain (1980). This model was found to be at the basis of all programmes in which this package is used. In brief, this model of communicative competence posits four interrelated competencies which come into play in effective communication: linguistic competence, discourse competence, socio-linguistic competence, and strategic competence. Each of these competencies has been considered in the elaboration of the various techniques and in the development of the evaluation scheme, including the global descriptions of performance levels which accompany these evaluation schemes. In this way MOCAP has respected the principle of construct validity.

The third and final point relates to the components of successful oral communication. MOCAP respects the principles of the communicative/ experiential syllabus as put forward by Tremblay *et al.*, (1990: 2,3) where the aim is "to provide learners with a chance to communicate in authentic communicative situations" where "all learning activities need to be structured around communicative tasks." Whereas providing authentic tasks within the confines of the second language classroom often involves compromises, MOCAP contains evaluation techniques which give students access to a wide range of communicative situations, provide for authentic language use with a focus on meaning rather than the form of language, involve students in the activities in a personal way, and provide exposure to different speakers in more and less formal situations. These techniques also take into account the varying degrees of difficulty found in both non-interactive and interactive situations (Tremblay *et al.*, 1990). Students at lower levels are engaged in activities that involve shorter messages, a focus on concrete topics, participation in social routines, and general sharing of information. At higher levels, students are involved in situations which require lengthy productions, deal with controversial and more wide-ranging topics, cause students to express a point of view and in some cases defend that point of view.

Teacher Input in the Development Process: Building upon a Solid Foundation

In the area of FSL education, department of education representatives identified as a priority the need for an evaluation instrument which would reflect a communicative/experiential approach to language teaching and which would serve teachers in all three provinces. It was agreed that what was needed most was an evaluation tool which could be put in the hands of classroom teachers to use for formative evaluation purposes; that is, as a means of assessing students' progress, diagnosing strengths and weaknesses in students' performance, and providing feedback to both students and teachers on the effectiveness of their learning and teaching. It was also recognised that this instrument should be adaptable to different situations, and that the scoring of the various tasks should be straightforward.

MOCAP was developed for use by classroom teachers who were involved in the writing of various evaluation tasks and in the piloting and implementation processes. Thirty teachers spanning all three provinces came together and worked in teams according to the level at which they taught. In addition to agreeing on particular themes and identifying relevant fields of experience, these teachers also spent considerable time reaching a consensus on what was appropriate and realistic to expect of students at a given level in terms of both language tasks and grammatical content. These language tasks and grammatical content are criterion-referenced insofar as they are based on lists taken from the curriculum guides for core French and French immersion language arts at both Grade 6 and Grade 9 in the Maritime provinces. The grammatical content was chosen in light of the language tasks and the level of the students involved. The developers recognised that various tasks could be accomplished with varying degrees of accuracy and sophistication depending upon the linguistic abilities of the students, and, therefore, it was not possible to indicate precisely what the grammatical content would be for any given communicative situation. However, the teachers felt that some indication of grammatical content that would likely be required to carry out a series of language tasks would be useful to MOCAP users. In this regard, both the specific language tasks and probable grammatical content involved in each variation of each technique are provided with the evaluation techniques.

The teacher resource team then created specific communicative situations which corresponded to the theme selected and which involved specific language tasks. Instructions to students and any ideas for props that may be required were also included. These formed the basis of the entire MOCAP. Guided in their work by evaluation specialists, teachers spent four complete days producing their draft versions. In addition to the classroom teachers who attended this workshop and subsequently served as a resource team, there was also a group of French second language coordinators from various school boards and consultants from the departments of education who assisted with the workshop and the field-testing process. This team approach to development of the instrument ensured widespread commitment to this style of evaluation, which represented a major departure from previous testing methods.

The tasks were revised, prepared for pilot testing, reanalysed in light of teacher and student reactions, piloted a second time, and then revised in their final format. Initial piloting involved all teachers who participated in the workshop described above. Examples of all variations of all techniques were sent to each teacher who experimented with these pilot items with a minimum of three groups of students for each version. This process was conducted over a period of 10 weeks. Teachers were also sent a survey which they completed in order to indicate their degree of agreement or disagreement with various aspects of the different techniques (appropriacy of content, difficulty of language, ease of scoring, and so forth). Subsequent to this first stage of piloting, changes were made to the various techniques according to the reactions of teachers and students involved. Any techniques which required major revision (i.e., not simply formatting or stylistic changes) were repiloted with a smaller sample of teacher and the results were integrated into the final version.

Portfolio Assessment in FSL: A Variety of Techniques

As noted above, there are in effect four versions of MOCAP – one version for each grade and programme: 6 core, 9 core, 6 immersion, 9 immersion. Three of the evaluation techniques are basically the same for all four levels – role plays, information gaps, discussion. Two other techniques vary from core to immersion with forms and describing pictures being used in core French and questionnaires and oral summaries being used in French immersion. The thematic content, language tasks, and linguistic content vary from one version to another. The following is a listing and description of the various evaluation techniques.

Describing pictures

This technique is designed for core French at both Grades 6 and 9. It consists of a series of illustrations that students are required to look at and talk about. This may take the form of description or narration or some combination of both. Essentially, students are instructed to look at a sequence of illustrations and to describe and/or narrate the content of these drawings. The teacher's involvement should be minimal in such situations. The student is allowed two minutes to examine the illustrations before beginning the activity. It should be recognised that pauses during the activity could be meaningful and eventually lead to productive expression, and teachers should only intervene where necessary to keep the activity going. The extent to which the teacher has to provide clues, ask questions and help the student will be reflected in the evaluation.

Oral summary

This technique is destined for use in French immersion classes at both grade levels. Students are required to listen to an oral, tape-recorded passage twice, and then, in their own words, give an account of the main points of the passage. Before listening to the passage which is recorded on audio-cassette (supplied in the assessment package), students are told that the purpose of this activity is for them to understand the principal elements of the oral passage and to reformulate these passages in their own words. Students are also told that they are not expected to remember secondary details. They are then reminded that the passage will be played twice. Again in this situation the teacher's involvement should be minimal. A question may be asked or a comment made to keep the activity going if the student is obviously stuck on a point, but otherwise the teacher's role should be passive.

Forms

This technique involves an interview between two students assisted by a form that one of the students must complete. These forms, which are supplied in the assessment package, may be applications for a summer camp, customs forms, and so forth that generally require factual information. The student who holds the form is the one who will be required to ask the question. It should be made clear to this student that the questions are not written in complete sentences, bur rather in point form. This student's task is to formulate the required questions and to ask these in a manner that the other student can understand. The second student must answer these questions to the best of his or her ability. It is not necessary for the first student to complete the form as it is only meant as a prop and an aid to the student in formulating questions.

Questionnaire

Similar to the forms above, this technique designed for use in immersion involves an interview between two students assisted by a form. In this case, in addition to factual information, the questionnaire which is supplied in the assessment package requires students to ask and respond to questions involving opinions, attitudes, and so on. The student who holds the questionnaire is the one who will be required to ask the questions. It should be made clear to this student that the questions are not written in complete sentences, but rather in point form. This student's task is to formulate the required questions and to ask these in a manner that the other student can understand. The second student must answer these questions to the best of his or her ability. It is not necessary for the first student to complete the questionnaire as it is only meant as a prop and an aid to the student in formulating questions.

Information gap

This technique, which is used in both core and immersion, involves two students working together in order to obtain the information required to complete a specific task. One student possesses a document containing the complete or accurate set of information that the other does not have. These documents are supplied in the assessment package and are given to students at the beginning of the evaluation session. In some cases, the actual transfer of information is sufficient to complete the task while in other situations students must use the new information to answer specific questions related to it. It should be made clear to both students that their general task is to work together to provide one another with any information that may be missing from their respective documents.

Role plays

This technique involves two students in a face-to-face encounter. The students are provided with the student documents before the role play which provide them with background information and specific instructions as to the information they must request and provide. The students are given two minutes to examine the document and to ensure they understand the instructions completely. They may ask questions of clarification, but should not be allowed to rehearse their part.

Discussion

This technique involves four students in a round-table type exchange. The students are provided with a document that provides background information and specific instructions as to the language tasks that they are expected to accomplish. Students are given two minutes to read the document so they can understand the instructions and formulate their ideas. They should not be allowed to rehearse, however. In core French the exchange takes the form of a conversation or question-and-answer session, whereas in immersion the event is much more debate-oriented. Students should be told before beginning that in order for the teacher to evaluate they all must participate in the discussion. With a group of four, the teacher may have to intervene in order to give less vocal students an opportunity to express themselves. It is also recommended that two teachers be involved in the evaluation of the group discussion as it is very difficult for one teacher to fairly evaluate four students simultaneously.

One of the distinguishing features of all the techniques (except *describing pictures and oral summaries*) is that the teacher acts as an observer who evaluates student-to-student interaction. The reason for this system is two-fold. First, one of the goals of evaluation is to assess authentic, meaningful communication; by removing herself/himself from the inter-action, the teacher is much more likely to elicit authentic speech samples from the students. Second, most teachers are using a variety of techniques for interactive groupwork (for example, cooperative learning) during their classes; by evaluating students in interactive situations, a teacher ensures that the assessment methods match classroom practice.

Evaluating Student Performance: Diagnostic and Global Assessment

It is extremely important that all students have the opportunity to practise and be familiar with a particular evaluation technique before being evaluated. If a student does not know what is generally expected in a role play situation of this type, then one cannot evaluate that student's performance in a valid way. It is also important for teachers to realise that the evaluation scheme which accompanies each technique may require some prior familiarisation. Teachers are encouraged to experiment with this evaluation scheme at the same time as students are involved in practice sessions in order to be familiar with its content and scoring format. It is also very important to remember that this evaluation package allows the student and the teacher to select from a variety of techniques in order to create a composite profile of the student's performance over an extended period of time. This aspect of portfolio assessment should not be over-looked when the time comes to make an evaluative judgement regarding a student's progress or achievement.

It was noted above that evaluation of communicative competence must reflect the principles of that theoretical model. The evaluation scheme developed for use with each of these techniques takes into account the various principles outlined above. An example of this scheme is presented and explained in detail below.

EVALUATION SHEET
ORAL SUMMARY (A)
GRADE 6 IMMERSION
THEME: *FOOD*

PUPIL _____ DATE_____

I. COMMUNICATION OF THE MESSAGE

A = Message communicated effectively and appropriately.
B = Message communicated but effectiveness and/or accuracy must
    be improved.
C = Message not communicated effectively.

Language tasks:	A	B	C
1. *Give information about location.*	☐	☐	☐
2. *Give numerical information.*	☐	☐	☐
3. *Give information about an event in the past.*	☐	☐	☐

II. DIAGNOSTIC ANALYSIS

Articulation: pronunciation; intonation; fluency _____
Facility: vocabulary (precision and variety); communicative strategies___
Grammaire: grammatical precision; discourse cohesion _____

III. GLOBAL EVALUATION   A☐   B☐   C☐
(See global descriptors in Appendix A)

Section I. With respect to language tasks, each task to be accomplished in a given evaluation technique is listed on the evaluation scheme which accompanies that technique. Teachers are asked to identify whether this task has been accomplished completely (A), in part (B), or not at all (C).

Section II. The scheme also allows for the measure of student progress and a diagnostic assessment of strengths and weaknesses. A section is provided for analysis of students' linguistic, socio-linguistic, discourse, and strategic competence and space is provided for the writing of specific comments with respect to student performance in these areas. In this section, teachers are requested to identify major strengths and weaknesses. Since one cannot evaluate everything nor can one diagnose each and every strength or weakness, the aim is to provide students with valuable feedback with respect to their progress (positive feedback), and one or two areas where they need to improve (negative feedback).

Section III. The evaluation scheme also allows for a global, holistic evaluation of student performance. This is arrived at by considering the evaluation with respect to the language tasks and individual competencies discussed above, and by comparing student performance to the descriptions provided of differing levels of competence – A, B, or C. These descriptions are located in Appendix A.

The evaluation scheme is designed to be "user-friendly" for classroom teachers. In addition to the letter grade (A, B, or C) for students' accomplishment of language tasks and their overall global performance, space is provided for teachers to write diagnostic comments, but these should be in point form and, as noted above, should be restricted to the main areas of students' strengths and weaknesses.

Conclusion: The Teaching/Testing Dilemma

This classroom-based evaluation format, as is the case for any other, will only be successful to the extent that it reflects the actual teaching practices that occur in the classrooms in which it is used. Classroom teachers from both core French and French immersion programmes have determined that these techniques are valid ways to evaluate student performance. These techniques reflect not only the content and objectives of curriculum guides but also, in many cases, the reality of classroom practice. However, there is the possibility that this evaluation format does not reflect the kind of teaching that goes on in certain classrooms. It is extremely important for us to respect the basic principle that evaluation and teaching are two complementary elements in the process of classroom instruction. If we consider this approach to assessment of students' performance to be worthwhile, we must likewise insist upon teaching practices which are consistent with this approach. It is clearly neither our intent nor our desire that this evaluation model be imposed upon teachers who are not ready or who have not been properly prepared to engage in such practices in their classrooms. Rather, we would hope that this evaluation package be presented as a model or as a goal for such teachers to work towards. In this way, teachers may gradually but steadily integrate communicative oral language activities in the daily teaching, and in the same way begin to use these communicative assessment techniques to evaluate the effectiveness of their teaching and their students' learning.

Appendix A

Global descriptors of levels of performance

Level A. The learner is almost always capable of using the language to carry out the target language tasks and does so in an appropriate manner. He/she almost always expresses him/herself with a superior level of grammatical precision. Pronunciation, intonation and flow never interfere with communication. The learner almost always understands without the need for repetition or reformulation. Communicative strategies such as gestures, requests for repetition, circumlocutions are almost always understandable, complete and naturally integrated into conversation. Discourse is logical and coherent. Discourse connectors such as pronouns and transitional words are used correctly and systematically.

Level B. The learner is often capable of using the language to carry out the target language tasks and often does so in an appropriate manner. He/she often expresses him/herself with an average level of grammatical precision. In general, pronunciation, intonation and flow never interfere with communication. The learner often understands without the need for repetition or reformulation. Communicative strategies such as gestures, requests for repetition, circumlocutions are often understandable, complete and naturally integrated into conversation. Discourse is often logical and coherent. Discourse connectors such as pronouns and transitional words are often used correctly and systematically.

Level C. The learner is often incapable of using the language to carry out the target language tasks. He/she expresses him/herself with little grammatical precision. Pronunciation, intonation and flow often interfere with communication. The learner does not understand without repetition or reformulation. Communicative strategies such as gestures, requests for repetition, circumlocutions are rarely used. Discourse is often illogical and incoherent. Discourse connectors such as pronouns and transitional words are rarely used correctly.

Appendix B

Student self-assessment questionnaire

Part 1 – Language tasks

Was I able to communicate all the messages and ideas involved in this activity?

YES☐ NO☐

If not, which messages or ideas was I not able to get across?

_____

Which messages or ideas did I find easiest to express? _____

What do I need to work on most? _____

In communicating these messages and ideas, was I able to use language that was suited to the specific situation (for example, did I use *tu* and *vous* appropriately; did I use slang expressions when it was not the right time or place?)

YES☐ NO☐

Part 2 – Specific strengths and areas needing work

Was I able to use the necessary vocabulary in order to participate in this activity?

YES☐ NO☐

If not, which words or expressions did I need to know that I was not able to come up with? _____

If I was unable to come up with certain words or expressions, how did I get around the problem (For example, did I use gestures, did I use English words or expressions, did I try to describe the object or event, or did I just try to avoid the topic?) _____

Was I able to say what I needed to say correctly (without making grammatical mistakes)?

YES☐ NO☐

If so, some examples of correct speech that I used are_____

If there were things that I said incorrectly, some examples of the kind of mistakes that I made with language are: _____

Did the way I pronounced certain words or groups of words cause any problems in getting my message across?
Yes ☐ No ☐

If yes, some examples of words or groups of words that I found hard to pronounce are _____

Part 3 – Global evaluation

Overall, I feel that my performance on this activity was (A) quite good ☐, (B) not bad ☐, (C) not up to par ☐.

References

Antonacci, P.A. (1993) Natural assessment in whole language classrooms. In A. Carrasquillo and C. Hedley (eds) *Whole Language and the Bilingual Learner* (pp. 116–31). Norwood, NJ: Ablex Publishing Company.

Belanoff, P. and Dickson, M. (1991) (eds) *Portfolios, Process and Product*. Portsmouth, NH: Boynton/Cook Publishers Heinemann.

Canale, M. and Swain, M. (1980) Theoretical bases for communicative approaches to second language teaching and testing. *Applied Linguistics* 1 (1), 1–47.

Leblanc, R. (1990) *National Core French Study. A Synthesis*. Ottawa: M Éditeur.

Tremblay, R., Duplantie, M. and Huot, D. (1990) *National Core French Study. The Communicative/Experiential Syllabus*. Ottawa: M Éditeur.

Index

Authors

Subjects